WALK BRITAIN

WALK BRITAIN

90 INSPIRATIONAL CAR-FREE WALKS IN ENGLAND, SCOTLAND AND WALES

First published in 2025 by Vertebrate Publishing.

VERTEBRATE PUBLISHING
Omega Court, 352 Cemetery Road, Sheffield S11 8FT, United Kingdom.
www.adventurebooks.com

Copyright © 2025 Elise Downing and Vertebrate Publishing Ltd.
Foreword copyright © 2025 Emily Chappell.

Elise Downing has asserted her rights under the Copyright,
Designs and Patents Act 1988 to be identified as author of this work.

A CIP catalogue record for this book is available from the British Library.

ISBN 978-1-83981-144-9 (Paperback)
ISBN 978-1-83981-145-6 (Ebook)

All rights reserved. No part of this work covered by the copyright herein may be reproduced or used in any form or by any means – graphic, electronic, or mechanised, including photocopying, recording, taping, or information storage and retrieval systems – without the written permission of the publisher.

Front cover: the Great Ridge, Peak District. © Sarah Lister
Back cover (L–R): Cleveland Way, North York Moors © Jon Barton; scrambling on Tryfan, Eryri/Snowdonia; Leith Hill Tower, Surrey Hills © Jane Beagley; West Highland Way, Western Highlands; South West Coast Path, Isle of Purbeck; sheep near High Street, Lake District; Glen Catacol, Isle of Arran; Embleton Bay, Northumberland.

Photography by Elise Downing unless otherwise credited.

 Maps reproduced by permission of Ordnance Survey on behalf of The Controller of His Majesty's Stationery Office. © Crown Copyright. AC0000809882

Overview map credit on page iv by Active Maps, www.activemaps.co.uk

Edited by Helen Parry; cover design, layout and production by Jane Beagley.
www.adventurebooks.com

Printed and bound in Slovenia by Latitude Press.

Vertebrate Publishing is committed to printing on paper from sustainable sources.

Every effort has been made to achieve accuracy of the information in this guidebook. The authors, publishers and copyright owners can take no responsibility for: loss or injury (including fatal) to persons; loss or damage to property or equipment; trespass, irresponsible behaviour or any other mishap that may be suffered as a result of following the route descriptions or advice offered in this guidebook. The inclusion of a track or path as part of a route, or otherwise recommended, in this guidebook does not guarantee that the track or path will remain a right of way. If conflict with landowners arises we advise that you act politely and leave by the shortest route available. If the matter needs to be taken further then please take it up with the relevant authority.

WALK BRITAIN

90 INSPIRATIONAL CAR-FREE WALKS IN
ENGLAND, SCOTLAND AND WALES

ELISE DOWNING

Vertebrate Publishing, Sheffield
www.adventurebooks.com

Foreword vii
Introduction ix
Walk Britain x
How to use this book xi
Planning a car-free adventure xii
Safety in the outdoors xiv

England & the Isles 1
Cornish Coast **1–5** 3
Dartmoor **6–10** 13
Jurassic Coast **11–15** 23
London Day Trips **16–20** 33
Norfolk Broads **21–25** 41
Peak District **26–30** 49
Yorkshire Dales **31–35** 59
Isle of Man **36–40** 69
Lake District **41–45** 79
North York Moors **46–50** 89
Northumberland **51–55** 97

Wales 105
Pembrokeshire **56–60** 107
Bannau Brycheiniog/Brecon Beacons **61–65** 117
Eryri/Snowdonia **66–70** 127

Scotland 135
Scottish Borders **71–75** 137
Isle of Arran **76–80** 145
Western Highlands **81–85** 155
Cairngorms **86–90** 167

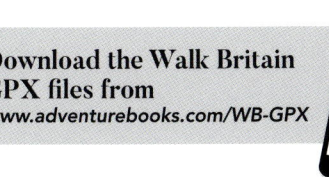
Download the Walk Britain GPX files from
www.adventurebooks.com/WB-GPX

komoot
www.komoot.com/collection/2452665

Opposite Devil's Ridge in the Western Highlands

Foreword

Almost everyone will encounter a few barriers when it comes to getting into the countryside. In some cases, these are very easily resolved. If all that's standing in your way is checking your map to find out where the trail starts, then you'll be out there in no time. But some people can nurse this ambition for years without finding a way of realising it – because of safety concerns, because they lack the skills and don't know where to get them, or because they've somehow been led to believe that the outdoors is not for them.

In my case the barrier was logistical. I knew I'd love walking in the hills, because I'd spent years exploring remote corners of the world by bike, racing across continents, and seeking out quiet Alpine meadows to camp in. Quite often, as I pedalled up the switchbacks towards a pass, I'd see people with backpacks and walking boots who were going even higher than me, for whom the pinnacle of my ride was merely their starting point. So, this was what a hiking holiday must look like, I thought to myself. I wanted to follow them and see what it was like up there – but I couldn't, because what would I do with the bike?

Back in the UK, I once or twice experimented with cycling to the bottom of a mountain, sleeping in my tent, and then hiding bike and camping gear while I hiked up and down. This worked, but it felt too risky and wasn't really practical. Most guidebooks were no help – they just told me where the car parks were, and this was irrelevant to me because I'd never learned to drive. So, I developed the conviction that hiking was only for proper grown-ups, and left them to it.

Little did I know that someone had read one of my periodic social media pleas for advice, and was busy working on a solution.

I first met Elise partway through her run round the UK coast, and was struck both by the magnitude of her expedition, and the modesty with which she went about it. She didn't seem to think she was anything special – but the rest of us felt differently, and watched with increasing admiration over the next few years, as she took on more running challenges, became an accomplished route-planner, and built herself a career as an author and speaker.

She may at some point have realised that she *is* something special, but I'm not so sure, because she still has the attitude that anyone else could do what she does, and puts considerable effort into showing them how. There are no secrets with Elise, as far as I can tell: if she discovers a useful hack, she'll share it with you; if she finds a good trail, she'll tell you about it; and if she figures out a way to get there and back using public transport, she'll definitely let you know.

Her generosity and enthusiasm have already inspired countless real-world adventures, and this book will launch many more. And you don't need to be a non-driver like me. *Walk Britain* will help you avoid overflowing car parks on a bank holiday. It'll show you how to plan adventures with a lower carbon footprint, and it'll mean you can enjoy as many post-walk pints as you like.

Following a recommendation from Elise, I once took the bus that runs between Kendal and Windermere. Almost everyone else on the top deck was dressed for a day out in the hills (I even saw a couple of ice axes), and before long I had got chatting to an old man. He asked where I was planning on going for my run, told me he had grown up not far from there, and spent the rest of the journey reminiscing about the decades he had spent in these hills that I was only just discovering.

I wouldn't have had that lovely encounter if I'd driven here, I thought, as I set off up the hill, already hoping I'd run into him again on my homeward journey.

Emily Chappell

Opposite Fairfield Horseshoe, Lake District © Angharad Caswell

Introduction

The idea for this book was born from a Twitter (now X) thread that Emily Chappell started back in April 2021.

> *The reason I don't do more hiking and mountain running is the difficulty of accessing trailheads without motorised transport …*
>
> *Reading the responses to this thread, it occurs to me that there is a very good market for a guidebook for car-free hiking/walking/trekking in the UK. Any publishers interested in commissioning one?*

I didn't have a driving licence at the time. My mum had offered to pay for a few driving lessons for my eighteenth birthday present, but I'd traded them in for an Interrail Pass (very on-brand for this book, now I think about it) and so, more than a decade later, all of my adventures were still car-free. I was desperate for the book Emily was suggesting to exist and immediately forwarded her Tweet to Kirsty Reade, commissioning editor at Vertebrate Publishing, with a plea something along the lines of: 'Please get Emily to write this book, I'll buy it.'

Sadly, Emily wasn't able to take on the project at the time which meant that I was lucky enough to end up with it (and she has kindly written the foreword). Although I have since learned to drive, it's still a topic I'm hugely passionate about.

I feel strongly that the UK is one of the best countries in the world for walking and running. We have so much variety packed into a relatively small area: rugged coast, towering mountains, expansive moorland, quaint country villages, truly excellent pubs. And while it might not be perfect, we actually have a pretty vast public transport system to access our countryside compared to some places. In contrast, I was shocked by how impossible it was to explore the Great Smoky Mountains without hiring a car when I visited America earlier this year.

There's no denying that you sacrifice a little bit of convenience when you decide to travel by public transport (mainly in the packing area as you can't just chuck every single thing you own into the car boot). Car-free adventures should be approached through the lens of what you gain though. It's reading your book on the train instead of sitting on the motorway, it's having a leisurely breakfast in your holiday cottage because you don't have to arrive at the trailhead at the crack of dawn to secure a parking spot, it's enjoying a post-walk pint of local ale without worrying about driving home.

Researching and writing this book was both a lot of fun and a little stressful. It felt like a big responsibility essentially saying to people: 'these places are great, and you should spend your precious annual leave and hard-earned cash visiting them.' But I truly believe that everywhere I've suggested is well worth visiting and, whether you can't drive or choose not to, I hope the following pages will facilitate some amazing adventures for you.

Elise

Walk Britain

The routes
In this book there are 90 different routes across England, Wales and Scotland that you can complete on foot without using a car. All the routes are accessible by public transport, whether that's walking straight from a major train station or using local bus or train services to pick up a more remote trail. The routes are split into 18 sections, each one covering a different location with one suggested base and five route ideas you can do from there.

I've chosen these routes to showcase the variety of options available. From the Cornish coast to the Western Highlands, big multi-day adventures to loops you can do before breakfast, circumnavigations of whole islands to point-to-point jaunts finishing at a pub, I hope that flicking through these pages will demonstrate just how much scope there is to explore Britain's wild places without having to get behind the wheel.

The hardest thing was deciding what to leave out – this book is by no means exhaustive. If you enjoyed a particular type of adventure in one location, rest assured you'll almost certainly find something similar elsewhere – there are some extra ideas on this at the end of every section.

Keep reading for more help on finding inspiration for your own car-free adventures.

Base locations
Once you've gone to the effort of getting yourself to a particular place, I want to make sure you can see as much of the area as possible. For this reason, I've structured each section around one 'base location' from which the routes are easily accessible.

There are three main criteria for the base locations:

» Straightforward connections by public transport to the rest of the country (e.g. on or near a mainline railway station).
» A good combination of routes you can do from the doorstep and/or using local public transport services to take you farther afield.
» A range of accommodation (to suit all price ranges) and places to buy food.

Rest assured that you won't be sent off on a one-a-day bus to a quaint village with no amenities within walking distance and only one good trail nearby! This means that occasionally I haven't been able to pick the *most* idyllic spot as a base in each area, as sometimes they don't go hand in hand with train stations and supermarkets. However, if you know that you aren't bothered about darting around all over the place trying different walks, then you might want to pick a route that really takes your fancy and base yourself near the start of that instead of in a more central location. For instance, Great Yarmouth is ideal for amenities and transport links to the Norfolk Broads but if you only particularly want to visit the seal colony I talk about in route 21, then you might want to stay in Winterton-on-Sea instead.

What this book isn't
Most importantly, this book isn't judgemental. It's not an all-or-nothing case against anybody ever owning a vehicle again (I do, so it would be rather hypocritical of me to tell you not to). And, given that a big part of my motivation for writing this book is to increase accessibility to the outdoors, it would be remiss of me not to acknowledge the often-prohibitive price of train tickets in Great Britain.

It may be the case, especially for families or groups, that completing your whole journey by public transport simply isn't practical.

However, I hope this book will show that, once you've arrived at your main destination, it's absolutely possible to leave your car at your accommodation and explore on foot and using local public transport for the remainder of your holiday. After all, I'm sure most of us would prefer to spend less of our free time sitting in traffic and more time enjoying a post-walk pint in the pub if we fancy it. More than 50 per cent of car journeys are for trips under five miles. By cutting out a few of these, we can make a real impact on congestion and pollution.

This book isn't intended to be prescriptive. I hope that the routes chosen will demonstrate the wealth of opportunities for car-free adventures in Great Britain and act as a jumping off point for planning your own, including ones starting from your very own doorstep (arguably the best place for a car-free adventure – see page xiii).

How to use this book

Each section starts with an introduction – here you'll find some handy information about what to expect in the area, what the base location is like, how to get there by public transport and a brief idea of the types of accommodation on offer.

Moving on, each route has details of the distance, metres of ascent, start and finish points, and how to get there by public transport, along with overview mapping and a route profile.

This book aims to offer inspiration more than instruction and, as such, the route descriptions focus on telling you *why* I think a certain route is worth checking out along with details of interesting things you might see along the way. I won't be telling you exactly how to execute the route (e.g. you won't find a lot of 'turn left here'). If you'd like to have a go at the routes, you can download the GPX files or take a look at the designated Komoot collection (see page v).

> The routes are organised by distance into the following categories:
> » **short:** up to 8 kilometres
> » **medium:** 9–16 kilometres
> » **long:** 17–24 kilometres
> » **challenge:** 25–40 kilometres
> » **multi-day:** over 40 kilometres

I've tried to include something for everybody in each section, so in many areas you'll find one route fitting every category. There aren't any filler choices – routes included for the sake of fitting a template – so in some places you might find I've left out one category and doubled up on another. When choosing an adventure please do pay attention to factors other than distance too, such as ascent and terrain. Kilometres are not made equal and shorter doesn't always mean easier. Where possible, alternative options are mentioned; for instance, if there's a way to shorten or extend a route or divide it into sections. Hopefully you'll find something you like!

Planning a car-free adventure

Car-free adventures can require a little extra planning. You may have to consider what to pack more carefully when you can't just throw everything plus the kitchen sink into the back of the car, and your plans will need to work around bus or train timetables.

> Research the local public transport before you go, and make sure you have downloaded any relevant apps and timetables ready for your trip. Here are some useful websites:
> » www.traveline.info
> » www.traveline.cymru
> » www.travelinescotland.com
> » www.seat61.com
> » www.thetrainline.com
> » www.splitmyfare.co.uk

Where to stay

I haven't included many specific suggestions for accommodation in this book as where you choose to stay will depend a lot on your budget and general holiday style. Where possible, all of the base locations are close to a variety of accommodation options from campsites to B&Bs and holiday cottages, as well as easy access to other amenities including shops, cafes, pubs and restaurants. The latter is something to consider carefully – proximity can be important when you are car-free – it's less easy to carry large shopping hauls home when walking or on the bus, and you might not want to be faced with an hour-long walk just to buy a pint of milk for your morning cup of tea. It's a good idea to book early when you can – more central options often get booked up quickly and it's trickier to expand your search without vehicle access.

When to go

One huge plus of car-free travel is lessening your impact on the local environment. Honeypot areas can get overrun with visitors at peak times and adding in lots of vehicles only exacerbates the problems. With this in mind, it's great to consider other ways to leave a positive trace on your travels and being mindful of when to visit popular spots is one way to do this. If you can, consider visiting at less busy times – midweek, outside of school holidays or during the cooler months.

There are lots of benefits to travelling off-peak when you can – and they're not all altruistic! You can experience the freedom of having a beauty spot all to yourself, rather than facing a queue for the summit. Accommodation will be cheaper, and buses and trains will be quieter. There's something exhilarating about being out and about on a brisk winter's day too, not to mention

1 Whernside, Yorkshire Three Peaks

the utter joy of putting some warm, dry socks on after being outside battling the elements.

On the flipside, do be aware that some bus services, cafes and accommodation are seasonal, so check before you travel.

Other things to think about

» If your accommodation is self-catered and not within easy reach of a shop, consider doing an online food order ahead of time to save lugging lots of heavy bags around on the train.
» Buses and trains are typically less frequent in rural areas. Make sure you've downloaded the latest timetables and bear in mind any alterations for weekends and bank holidays. I once got caught out by this on the Pembrokeshire coast and it resulted in a very expensive taxi!
» Look into kit hire at your destination for things like paddleboards and bikes. Similarly, some campsites have pre-erected tents or camping huts which could save you some luggage.
» If you're travelling by train and bringing a bike, make sure you've booked it in ahead of time if necessary.
» Invest in a water filter bottle which allows you to fill up basically anywhere and means you don't have to lug excess water weight around.

Doorstep adventures

The routes in this book are really just suggestions and show how you can explore some of Great Britain's most iconic adventure hubs without a car. But there are literally thousands more car-free adventures out there for you to go on – and some of the best of these will start right on your doorstep.

I love a point-to-point adventure, either starting from or finishing at home. Choose a destination that you know is a simple train or bus ride away then have some fun with a map, working out the best footpaths and trails to connect to get you there. Komoot's route planner is a good tool to help you out too – it works a bit like Google Maps but includes footpaths and you can see the make-up of your route in terms of surface types, with estimated timings specific to the terrain.

Another idea is to connect up some specific destinations in your immediate vicinity. It could be anything you're interested in – 16th-century churches, real ale pubs, tea shops, parks, streets with a festive themed name for a Christmas adventure (if you're thinking that's a bit niche then you're right, but it's one I've actually done). Mark them out on a map and see if you can create a loop to travel round them on foot.

Or perhaps there's a long-distance trail close by that you could chip away at in chunks, taking buses to your start and end points? What about hunting down the high and low points in your county? Can you go for multiple modes of travel in one day, cycling to the bottom of a hill, hiking up and then cycling home again?

How to find routes

There are some fantastic resources out there for finding new routes to try. Most navigation apps (such as Komoot, OS Maps and AllTrails) have 'discover' sections and some allow you to specifically filter by tours which are accessible by public transport. If there's a specific spot you want to see which seems inaccessible, zoom out a bit and look at ways you could extend the route if you're happy to walk a little further or perhaps turn it into a two-day trip. I often find that working out a way to tackle a route car-free actually adds to the adventure, and can take you to places you otherwise may have skipped right past.

Safety in the outdoors

Weather
Check the weather forecast before you set off, so you'll be aware of what conditions to expect. Don't totally rely on it though; always carry a waterproof and a spare layer, in case you have to stop.
www.metoffice.gov.uk
www.mwis.org.uk

Navigation
The mapping and GPX files included in this book are intended for planning and information; you will need to use additional mapping and navigation methods while walking: either a good quality online mapping app (such as Komoot, OS Maps, Gaia GPS, OutdoorActive or Topo GPS) on a mobile phone or GPS unit, or a hard-copy map and compass. Both require practice; understanding maps and symbols and orienting yourself from them is a useful skill to learn; there are many tutorial videos online that can help with this. Always carry a hard-copy map as a back-up in case your GPS device fails.

Preparation
Preparation will make the trail much more enjoyable. Practise carrying your intended load before setting off, and make sure you've worn your boots and tried your navigation aids in advance. Read up on the route, choose a walk that is within your capabilities and experience, and try to be flexible if weather, health or fitness means a change of plan becomes necessary. The routes in this book are extremely varied in difficulty; some are well waymarked and follow good paths throughout; others are less obvious to navigate, and you will need to be prepared for the rigours of remote and exposed terrain.

The AdventureSmart website is a great resource for learning more about safety in the outdoors: www.adventuresmart.uk

Rescue
Always notify someone of your plans and expected schedule before you start. In the event of an accident or emergency call **999** (or **112**) and ask for POLICE and then (if you are in a remote area) MOUNTAIN RESCUE.

Where possible give a six-figure grid reference for your location or that of the casualty.

In locations where your phone signal is poor or absent it is sometimes possible to send an emergency SMS if you have pre-registered your phone with www.emergencysms.net

In the absence of any phone signal, you should blow a whistle to attract attention, using six consecutive blasts, repeated once a minute.

Environment
As responsible outdoor enthusiasts it is important that we minimise our impact on the environment we walk through. Best practice includes sticking to the main trail where possible and avoiding shortcuts in popular areas where maintained trails are provided (for example, don't cut the corners off a zigzagging trail). This is to reduce surrounding soil erosion and prevent the gradual formation of duplicate trails across the landscape.

Leave only footprints wherever you walk. Take all litter home with you and remember that even some biodegradable waste (such as banana skins or orange peel) takes a very long time to decompose and is unsightly for others.

If your walk involves overnighting in a refuges or bothy, make sure you follow the Bothy Code: www.mountainbothies.org.uk Only wild camp where permitted to do so, and make sure you leave no trace.

Do not make or cause any fires anywhere in the landscape (avoid moving rocks for firepits, damaging trees for firewood or burning fragile upland soils and vegetation). Burned logs and

SAFETY IN THE OUTDOORS

1 Blorenge, Bannau Brycheiniog/Brecon Beacons

fire debris are unsightly and scorched ground takes years to recover. Instead use a camping stove which does not transfer heat to the ground.

In remote locations, where there is no access to toilet facilities, make sure that you find somewhere away from the trail and dig a hole 15 centimetres deep. This should be somewhere at least 30 metres away from water and not in a place that others might use (for example, climbers, wild campers or exploring children). If you use toilet paper, burn it or take it away with you – don't bury it or leave it under rocks. In popular areas where such a location is not available, double-bag your waste and carry it out with you. The same applies for all sanitary products.

Access

The regulations around land access vary across Great Britain – the following tips and resources should help:
  » Respect access restrictions and understand which areas are Open Access Land in England and Wales:
  www.gov.uk/right-of-way-open-access-land
  www.naturalresources.wales/days-out/places-to-visit
  » Always follow the Countryside Code:
  www.gov.uk/government/publications/the-countryside-code
  » In Scotland, where walkers have a right to responsible access, ensure you follow the Scottish Outdoor Access Code:
  www.outdooraccess-scotland.scot

Close gates behind you and do not climb drystone walls or bend wire fences. If you walk with a dog, be mindful of livestock and wildlife.

Hazards

Ticks, which can spread the serious infection causing Lyme disease, are present across Great Britain. Check yourself at least once a day for these tiny bloodsuckers, and carry a pair of tick removal tweezers. If you develop the telltale bull's-eye-shaped rash or cold symptoms after a bite, seek medical advice. Wearing long sleeves and trousers, and avoiding bashing through bracken will help minimise the chances of a bite. For more information see *www.lymediseaseaction.org.uk*

Midges are an occupational hazard of walking in summer, particularly in Scotland. They vanish in even the slightest breeze, but on still, warm and damp days these tiny biting insects can become unbearable if you are unprepared. Take repellent, cover up and consider taking a midge net to keep them off your face, especially if camping in Scotland between June and September.

ENGLAND & THE ISLES

Cornish Coast 3
1 Mousehole to Lamorna 4
2 History and Hills Loop 5
3 Marazion to Porthleven 6
4 St Ives to Sennen Cove 8
5 Cornish Celtic Way 10

Dartmoor 13
6 East Hill 14
7 Belstone Loop 15
8 High Willhays and Meldon Reservoir 16
9 Okehampton to Tavistock 18
10 Two Moors Way 20

Jurassic Coast 23
11 Durlston Country Park and Anvil Point 24
12 Old Harry Rocks 25
13 Worth Matravers and the Priest's Way 26
14 Corfe Castle 28
15 Jurassic Coast Path 30

London Day Trips 33
16 Epping Forest 34
17 Chilterns 35
18 South Downs 36
19 Hoo Peninsula 37
20 Surrey Hills 38

Norfolk Broads 41
21 Winterton Circular 42
22 Berney Marshes 43
23 Acle to Great Yarmouth 44
24 Great Yarmouth to Oulton Broad 45
25 Wherryman's Way 46

Peak District 49
26 Ladybower Reservoir 50
27 Mam Tor 51
28 Stanage and Burbage Edges 52
29 Edale Skyline 54
30 Pennine Way 56

Yorkshire Dales 59
31 Warrendale Knotts and Attermire Scar 60
32 Whernside and the Ribblehead Viaduct 61
33 Settle to Ribblehead 62
34 Yorkshire Three Peaks 64
35 Dales Way 66

Isle of Man 69
36 Dhoon Glen 70
37 Snaefell 71
38 Calf of Man Circular 72
39 Peel to Port Erin 74
40 Raad ny Foillan 76

Lake District 79
41 Orrest Head 80
42 Grasmere and Rydal Water 81
43 Fairfield Horseshoe 82
44 Windermere to Penrith over High Street 84
45 Cumbria Way 86

North York Moors 89
46 Grosmont to Goathland 90
47 Roseberry Topping 91
48 Fryup Dales and Danby Beacon 92
49 Esk Valley 93
50 Cleveland Way 94

Northumberland 97
51 Alnmouth and the River Aln 98
52 Dunstanburgh Castle 99
53 Simonside Hills 100
54 Alnmouth to Bamburgh 101
55 Northumberland Coast Path 102

Opposite On the Cleveland Way near Robin Hood's Bay
© Jon Barton

ENGLAND & THE ISLES

Cornish Coast

BASE LOCATION **Penzance**

WHERE TO STAY **Wide variety of B&Bs and self-catering options in Penzance, plus YHA Penzance (2km from Penzance railway station; local buses available). Closest campsite is Ponsandane (summer only, 1km from station).**

HOW TO GET THERE **By train to Penzance. Direct line from London or change in Bristol or Birmingham for connections to the North.**

It's hard to put your finger on what exactly makes Cornwall so special. Sitting at the very south-western tip of the country, there's no denying that it can be a bit of a faff to get there from many areas further north, especially as the motorway only goes as far as Exeter, 60 kilometres from the Cornish border. Luckily the train goes a little farther and will take you to the western corner of the county, with sleeper services even available from London.

And once you're there, I'm certain that every hour spent on the train will have felt worth it. Here's just a tiny fraction of what you can expect to enjoy on the Cornish coast: rugged coast paths, clear blue water, unique customs, strong communities, postcard-worthy fishing villages, mouth-watering local produce, some of the best beaches in the world, cream teas, pasties, lush green landscapes, wild flowers, seals, seabirds … the list truly does go on and on. I'm sure once you've visited, you'll have many more things to add to it.

Unsurprisingly, the routes in this chapter largely centre around the coast which is undoubtedly Cornwall's biggest attraction. I'll take you inland too though, giving you the chance to follow in the footsteps of pilgrims and explore sacred sites. Whichever route you choose to do, I recommend taking your time. One of the most wonderful things about Cornwall is the slower pace of life, which feels almost palpable as soon as you step off the train.

Penzance will be our base for this section, mainly for the purpose of showcasing a variety of routes. It might not be quite as picturesque as some of the tiny fishing villages you're used to associating with Cornwall, but it's got excellent public transport links, so you can get around easily and see more of the area. If you're less bothered about darting around, try picking the route you like the sound of best and base yourself near that instead (for example, Porthleven is lovely, with great coastal walking). If you do stay in Penzance, check out Jubilee Pool, the UK's only geothermal seawater lido.

1 Walking between Pendeen Watch and Zennor © Peter Turner Photography/Shutterstock.com
2 St Ives © Marcel van den Bos/Shutterstock.com 3 Coastal path at Zennor © Holly Auchincloss/Shutterstock.com
4 Mousehole Harbour © Ian Woolcock/Shutterstock.com 5 Coastline near Sennen Cove © Jon Barton
6 Pendeen Watch from Geevor Tin Mine © Roger Driscoll/Shutterstock.com

1 Lamorna Cove © Pajor Pawel/Shutterstock.com   2 Ding Dong Mine © Ian Woolcock/Shutterstock.com

1 Mousehole to Lamorna

CATEGORY **Short**   DISTANCE **8km**   ASCENT **170m**   START/FINISH **Mousehole**   PUBLIC TRANSPORT
Both ways: buses between Penzance bus station and The Old Coastguard, Mousehole (20 minutes)
MORE INFORMATION www.southwestcoastpath.org.uk

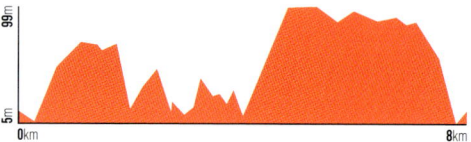

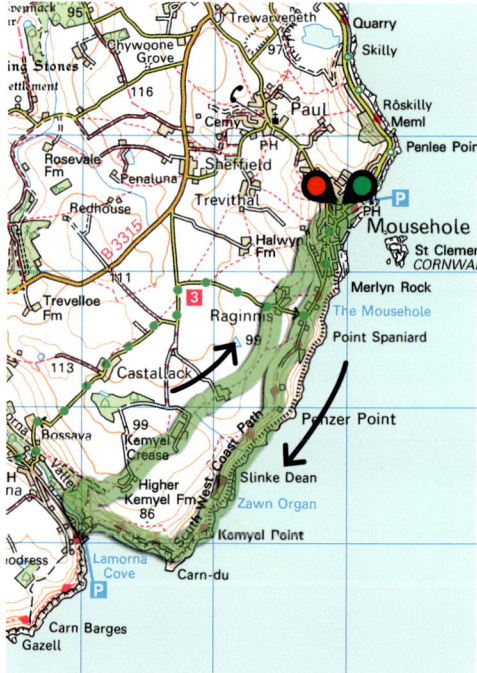

Mousehole is 5 kilometres from Penzance and while you could walk there, it's not the most exciting bit of coast so I'd recommend getting the bus and saving your energy for the more inspiring trails which take you further south. Mousehole itself is an interesting place known for, amongst other things, reputedly being named after a cave the size of a large mouse and the place from which starry gazey pie originates, an unusual delicacy which involves fish heads sticking out of a pastry crust. Not for the fainthearted visually, starry gazey pie is served up each year on the 23rd of December; Rick Stein has a recipe if you fancy trying it at home.

Small caves and large pies aside, Mousehole is the starting point for this walk out to Lamorna and back. The coast path goes through the Kemyel Crease Nature Reserve, taking you beneath a canopy of low branches. In the summer especially, this area is rich in fungi including the impressive earthstar mushroom. At Lamorna Cove you can stop at the cafe for a snack before heading back to Mousehole (good cakes and cream teas) or the sheltered cove makes it a good stop for a dip. The return to Mousehole is via clifftop trails through farmers' fields overlooking St Michael's Mount.

ENGLAND & THE ISLES

2 History and Hills Loop

CATEGORY **Medium**   DISTANCE **13km**   ASCENT **280m**   START/FINISH **Gurnard's Head Hotel, Porthmeor**
PUBLIC TRANSPORT **Both ways: buses between Penzance and Gurnard's Head Hotel, Porthmeor (30 minutes)**

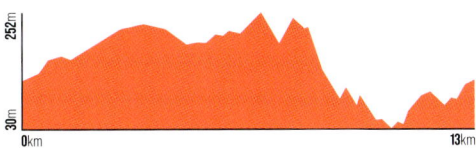

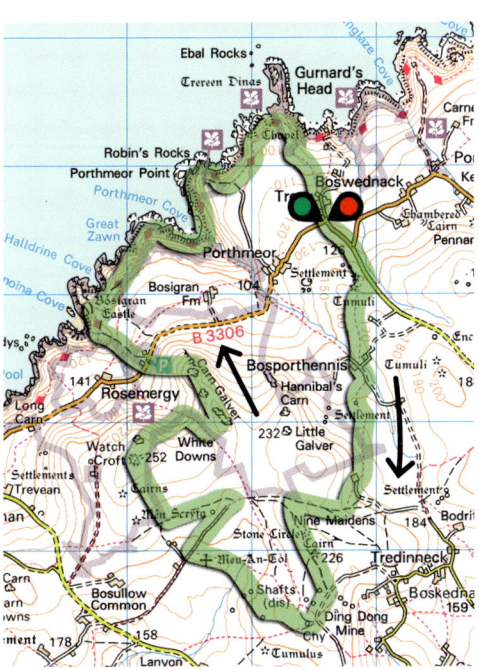

Take the bus to Gurnard's Head Hotel to begin, then from there it's really just a case of working your way through the long tick list of sights on this walk. Heading clockwise you'll first pass what was once Bosporthennis Sacred Well, known for its healing properties (admittedly it currently just looks like a damp patch in the ground, as it's in the process of being restored). From here the sights get a little more obvious and impressive: Nine Maidens Stone Circle, the Ding Dong Mine, Mên-an-tol rocks, Watch Croft hill and Carn Galver Mine. At 252 metres, Watch Croft qualifies as one of only five Marilyns (summits with an independent peak – or prominence – of at least 150 metres) in Cornwall and gives you a fantastic vantage point over the rest of the peninsula. It's a chance to really appreciate why this area deserves its National Landscape status, with views across Mount's Bay to the Lizard.

To complete your circuit, you'll drop down to Bosigran Castle on the coast path and follow it north to Gurnard's Head, before heading inland once more. The bus stop is conveniently located right by Gurnard's Head Hotel, winner of various awards and a good spot for lunch.

Cornwall might be best known for its coastline, but the National Landscape stretches to cover lots of inland ground too. This includes West Penwith, the area around the Land's End peninsula which hugs Penzance. Venture inland a little and you'll find granite moorland hills, medieval farmland and a huge array of megalithic monuments, which this route allows you to explore a good selection of.

WALK BRITAIN

1 St Michael's Mount © travellight/Shutterstock.com   2 Rinsey Head © Helen Hotson/Shutterstock.com
3 Prussia Cove © Ian Woolcock/Shutterstock.com   4 Sea thrift near Porthleven © Ian Woolcock/Shutterstock.com
5 Heading towards Porthleven © Peter Turner Photography/Shutterstock.com

3 Marazion to Porthleven

CATEGORY **Long**   DISTANCE **17km**   ASCENT **260m**
START **Marazion**   FINISH **Porthleven**   PUBLIC TRANSPORT **Outbound: bus from Penzance Interchange to Marazion Square (15 minutes). Return: bus from Porthleven Harbour to Penzance Interchange (45 minutes).**   MORE INFORMATION **www.southwestcoastpath.org.uk**

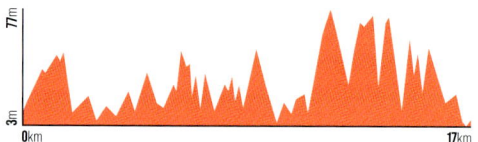

There are a few things that probably spring to mind when you think of the Cornish coast: quaint fishing villages, rocky headlands, dazzlingly blue water, rugged coast path and sandy beaches. This stretch of coastline between Marazion and Porthleven gives you them all. It's ideal if you can time it for a sunny day in the early spring or late autumn, when the trails will be quieter and the temperatures cooler but the scenery just as spectacular. Even better if you can get up early and see it all through the lens of glorious morning light. Don't worry if you don't manage to dial in the perfect weather though, this will still be a memorable day out, gulping down sea air and with the wind in your hair.

This is a relatively gentle section of the Cornish coast without *too* much climbing (go and check out the St Ives to Sennen Cove walk (route 4) if you want more ascent as it'll be delivered in bucketloads). As you depart from Marazion, you'll be following in the footsteps of your ancestors, as the historic town is reported to be the oldest settlement in Britain dating from 308 BC. On the way to Prussia Cove, the infamous smugglers' port, you'll pass numerous gorgeous beaches and quiet coves. In late summer, you'll be treated to purple heather and wild flowers covering the cliffs.

Heading into Porthleven, the cliffs change from granite to slate, and the path gets a little more rugged as the end looms closer. Porthleven is known for two things: its thriving art scene and fantastic food. Try and finish your walk or run early enough to make the most of both by looking around some of the galleries and craft shops either before or after refuelling. Foodwise, the Mussel Shoal is a great spot if you like seafood and Nauti But Ice is the place to go for ice cream.

WALK BRITAIN

1 Coastline near Sennen Cove © Jon Barton

4 St Ives to Sennen Cove

CATEGORY **Challenge**   DISTANCE **36km**   ASCENT **710m**   START **St Ives**   FINISH **Sennen Cove**   PUBLIC TRANSPORT **Outbound: train from Penzance to St Ives (one change; 45 minutes). Return: bus from Sennen Cove to Penzance Interchange (1 hour 30 minutes).**   MORE INFORMATION **www.southwestcoastpath.org.uk**

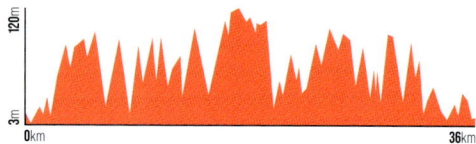

This 36-kilometre stretch of coast path takes you over some of the toughest ground you'll find on the entire South West Coast Path. The official trail website describes parts of it as a 'strenuous journey of roller coaster climbs' and I'll admit that this does ring true from when I most recently walked this route, on a gloriously sunny July day. But the difficulty of the terrain only adds to the experience.

Leaving busy St Ives behind, and it can be very busy – you'll need to sharpen your elbows if you want to get a Cornish pasty during peak times – it won't be long before you're into remote ground. The area around wild Zennor is a particular highlight of the route. It's equally beautiful whether you visit during the summer like I did, on a brisk winter's day or in the spring when the wild flowers are out in force.

Keep an eye out for seals as you approach the golden sands of Whitesand Bay and Sennen Cove and soak in the last moments of your adventure before catching the bus back from Sennen Cove. You can continue on for another couple of kilometres if you want to visit Land's End, but be warned the attraction might be a slightly jarring experience after the day of wilderness you've just experienced. The exception is if you visit midweek in the middle of winter as I did once, when you're almost guaranteed to have it to yourself and can enjoy the thrill of briefly being the most south-westerly person in England (and take a selfie by the Land's End sign without any onlookers).

1 The Lanherne Cross at St Mawgan © Penny Marns   2 Talland Bay © British Pilgrimage Trust

5 Cornish Celtic Way

CATEGORY **Multi-day**   DISTANCE **200km**   ASCENT **3,240m**   START **St Germans**   FINISH **St Michael's Mount**
PUBLIC TRANSPORT **Outbound: start at St Germans railway station (15 minutes from the mainline services at Plymouth). Return: onward trains from Penzance (6km from St Michael's Mount).**   MORE INFORMATION **www.cornishcelticway.co.uk**

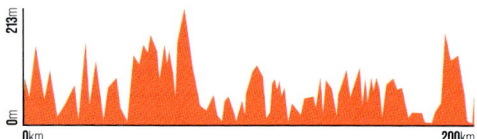

Perhaps the more obvious choice for this section's long-distance trail would have been the Cornwall Coast Path, which, at around 480 kilometres, forms nearly half of the full South West Coast Path. I absolutely would recommend this if you're looking for a fantastic adventure by the sea. I did it in January during one of the wettest winters on record in the UK and still had a genuinely epic month (though if I take my rose-tinted glasses off, I think I did also spend a lot of time complaining about having wet feet). Anyway, I suppose this preamble is my way of still including it.

But as soon as I learned about the Cornish Celtic Way, I loved the whole concept of it and knew I wanted to feature it. At 200 kilometres long, for most of us it's a more manageable distance for a week's or fortnight's holiday. A large portion of the route, which starts in St Germans near Plymouth and ends at St Michael's Mount near Penzance, follows the coast anyway, so you'll still get plenty of miles of coast path in your legs. You'll also have the added bonus of experiencing some fantastic inland sections too and following two established pilgrimage routes, The Saints' Way and St Michael's Way.

The Cornish Celtic Way was dreamed up by Reverend Nigel Marns; he was inspired by how Celtic saints engaged with nature and believed an understanding of God is revealed through it. Those of us who are more secularly minded shouldn't be put off though, the guidebook Marns has written for the route really just encourages you to experience a through-hike in a slightly more thoughtful way. The book is actually a key attraction of the trail, in my opinion. From beginning with an instruction to pick up a pebble at the start of the walk to mark your journey and then including various questions for contemplation, I think this will appeal to anybody who's interested in the history of the area and who is after more than just a route-march. There's also a Cornish Celtic Way passport that gives you access to budget accommodation on church floors along the way, and can be stamped as a memento of your journey.

If you liked this
The places I've talked about in this section make up just a tiny part of the Cornish coast, which is around 480 kilometres long in total. Try taking the train to St Austell or Falmouth and exploring the areas around those towns next time. Another idea is to take the ferry from Penzance over to the Isles of Scilly, described as 'An archipelago made for walking' by their tourist board.

Dartmoor

BASE LOCATION **Okehampton**

WHERE TO STAY **A range of options in Okehampton plus YHA Okehampton, which is right next to the town's railway station and also has a campsite. Otherwise, the closest campsite is at Sourton Down (15 minutes by bus from the centre of Okehampton).**

HOW TO GET THERE **By train to Okehampton (services from Exeter)**

I'm sure that it'll go down as one of my biggest regrets in life that I spent three years living in Plymouth, only a few miles south of Dartmoor, and yet somehow never visited. This national park covers 954 square kilometres and is home to 1,500 wild ponies, 40 kilometres of rivers and 160 tors (free-standing rock formations, sometimes also known as 'castle koppies', which I'd argue is a much more exciting name). You can even find the world's largest land slug, the ash black slug, lurking in the woodland.

I don't think anybody would argue with Dartmoor's suitability for an adventure. From its open moorland to its deep wooded valleys, it's a wild and expansive place with endless seemingly untouched spots for you to lose yourself in (hopefully not literally but navigation on Dartmoor can be tricky, so let this be your warning to keep your GPS device charged and your map and compass close). It's also the only place in England where you are legally allowed to wild camp, a right which it feels important to make the most of after we nearly lost it in 2023 (but has now been reinstated thanks to campaigning). For more information, see www.dartmoor.gov.uk/enjoy-dartmoor/outdoor-activities/camping

Yet I nearly discounted Dartmoor from this book as, back when I first started researching it, it seemed too awkward to access by public transport. Luckily that's changed now thanks to the recent reopening of the Dartmoor Line which takes you from Exeter to Okehampton on the northern edge of the national park. And you're in for a treat even before you get out on to the trails, with Okehampton station being home to a fantastic cafe and a bookshop, plus a YHA and bike hire on-site. When you're done hanging out at the train station, you'll find the trails on to the moor just a stone's throw away.

1 High Willhays **2** Golden hour on Dartmoor **3** Belstone **4** Rowtor
5 High Willhays **6** Lynmouth, North Devon (Two Moors Way) © Helen Parry

WALK BRITAIN

1 Okehampton station © JennyMB/Shutterstock.com   2 East Okement River

6 East Hill

CATEGORY **Short**   DISTANCE **4km**   ASCENT **140m**   START/FINISH **Okehampton station**
PUBLIC TRANSPORT **At the start. The station is a 15-minute walk or short bus ride from the centre of Okehampton.**

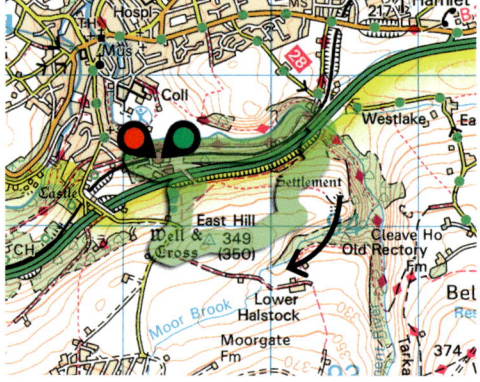

I think I might be Okehampton station's number one fan at this point — perhaps my favourite thing about it is just how close it is to where all the good stuff happens. Step off the train and within a matter of metres you're surrounded by greenery and nature, having barely had to step foot on a road. This route is the perfect example of that in action.

It's only 4 kilometres in length but within a relatively petite walk you get a bit of everything. First follow the Tramlines Bridleway for a short stretch before crossing the railway and heading up to East Hill. Being situated right on the Dartmoor border gives you panoramic views to some of the national park's taller peaks. This walk is delightful in its own right or is the perfect taster ahead of some bigger adventures.

What's most special about East Hill though — and the reason I'd really urge you to visit in the spring — is that at this time of the year you'll find a thick blanket of bluebells covering the rounded summit. Bluebells are an important wild flower in mythology and are often associated with dark fairy magic, so see if you can sense any strange happenings going on around you while you enjoy the views.

ENGLAND & THE ISLES

7 Belstone Loop

CATEGORY **Medium**   DISTANCE **11km**   ASCENT **300m**   START/FINISH **Okehampton station**   PUBLIC TRANSPORT **At the start. The station is a 15-minute walk or short bus ride from the centre of Okehampton.**

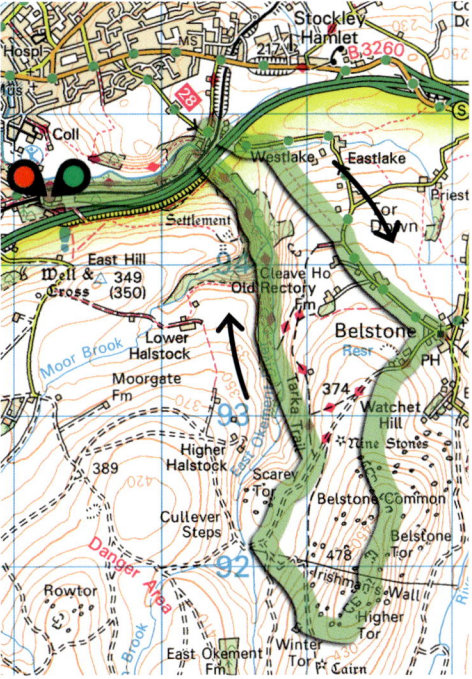

Belstone is the sort of village you'd find in one of those twee Christmas romance novels, except in this case it actually exists. One glance at the village website shows that there's a huge amount going on for permanent residents and this community feel only makes it a nicer place to visit too. It's a popular spot thanks to its location on the edge of the northern part of Dartmoor, in between two steep-sided valleys.

This varied route takes you to Belstone from Okehampton, first by following the Tramlines Bridleway. The rugged woodland trail takes you past an impressive waterfall before you climb up on to open pasture and then take the lane into Belstone. In the village, you'll often find various cows, ponies and sheep mooching around – as I discovered over some chips in the garden of The Tors, a self-described 'proper pub'. On weekend afternoons you can also stop by The Old School Tearoom for an afternoon tea to fuel the rest of your walk.

It's the second part of this walk where things get exciting, as you head on to the moor proper and climb up and around several tors: Belstone (the village's namesake), Winter and Scarey (one for Halloween?), plus Halstock Hill. You then follow quiet lanes back to Okehampton which is an absolute delight at golden hour, with the first inklings of sunset ahead of you. Our route finishes at the station but an extra kilometre will take you into the centre of Okehampton.

1 Meldon Reservoir

8 High Willhays and Meldon Reservoir

CATEGORY **Long**   DISTANCE **18km**
ASCENT **440m**   START/FINISH **Okehampton station**
PUBLIC TRANSPORT **At the start. The station is a 15-minute walk or short bus ride from the centre of Okehampton.**

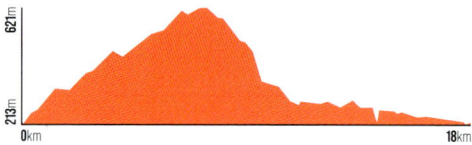

One of the most distinctive sights as you explore Dartmoor are the many tors you'll walk up, down and around. I'm a little ashamed to say that until I ran this route, I was ignorant to the fact that a 'tor' isn't just another word for 'hill'. I was merrily raving about my trot up High Willhays, referring to it as 'Dartmoor's tallest tor', when somebody kindly corrected me – that accolade actually belongs to Vixen Tor. This is because 'tor' specifically refers to the rocky formation on top of the hill, rather than the hill itself. Just clearing that up in case anybody else is as ignorant as I was …

Anyway, vocabulary lesson over and on to the route; I was lucky enough to do this on a bright, sunny day and it was an absolute corker. High Willhays might not boast the tallest stack of rocks, but its 621-metre height makes it the highest point on Dartmoor and in South West England. Along with the neighbouring Yes Tor (which you'll also visit on this route) they make up two of the three English peaks south of the Peak District which are over 610 metres.

Facts and figures are all well and good but what we really care about is what it's like on the ground; basically what I'm trying to say is that the stature of these two peaks makes them unparalleled in terms of the views they offer. Standing atop either hill you'll likely be surrounded by cattle grazing peacefully and Dartmoor ponies frolicking around. A word of warning – it can get windy up here due to how exposed it is. In bad weather you'll also only want to head out if you're a confident navigator as it is notoriously easy to get lost on Dartmoor.

After climbing the tors you'll drop down to the West Okement River and follow it to Meldon Reservoir. Sitting at nearly 300 metres above sea level, nestled in the Okehampton Valley and surrounded on all sides by steep banks, the reservoir offers one of those landscapes that even the very worst photographer will find it difficult to take a bad photo of. If you manage to prize your eyes away from the scenery in front of you and glance down, you might be lucky enough to see an adder or a grass snake darting in front of you.

From the reservoir you'll pick up the Granite Way to get you back to Okehampton. This traffic-free path for walkers and cyclists doesn't necessarily make for the most interesting walking but it does allow you to go over the stunning Meldon Viaduct which isn't to be missed. The last couple of kilometres are gentle at least, and soon you'll be back in Okehampton (armed with your new knowledge of tors).

1 Sourton   2 West Devon Way

9 Okehampton to Tavistock

CATEGORY **Challenge**   DISTANCE **31km**
ASCENT **450m**   START **Okehampton station**
FINISH **Tavistock**   PUBLIC TRANSPORT **Outbound:**
Okehampton station is a 15-minute walk or short bus ride from the centre of Okehampton. Return: bus from Tavistock to Okehampton (50 minutes).

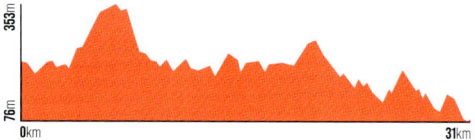

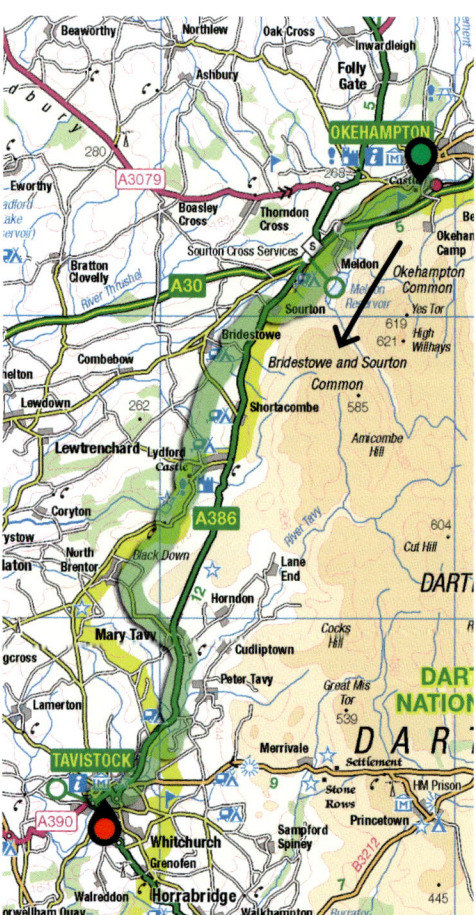

In its entirety, the West Devon Way is a 60-kilometre trail linking Okehampton with Plymouth. It is divided into eight stages and was specifically designed around local public transport services, ensuring you can access the start and end of each section without using a car. The northern part of the route takes you from Okehampton to Tavistock, skirting around the western edge of Dartmoor for 31 kilometres. It's a relatively low-level route passing through Sourton, Lydford and Mary Tavy, often sharing trails with the Dartmoor Way (which circumnavigates the entire moor and is worth checking out for a bigger adventure).

You've got a few key sights to look out for along the way, from Lydford's two Norman castles and famous gorge to the abandoned Wheal Fanny Copper Mine and the Grade II listed Harford Bridge. But perhaps the most distinctive thing to look out for on this route is The Highwayman Inn in Sourton, reputed to be the most unusual pub in Britain. I'm almost hesitant to tell you too much more but having now visited, I'd agree with that accolade. It has to be seen (and experienced) to be believed, really.

10 Two Moors Way

CATEGORY **Multi-day** DISTANCE **173km** ASCENT **3,450m** START **Wembury** FINISH **Lynmouth** PUBLIC TRANSPORT **Outbound: bus from Plymouth station to Wembury. Return: bus from Lynmouth to Barnstaple station.** MORE INFORMATION **www.twomoorsway.org**

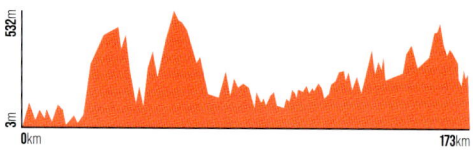

I first learned about the Two Moors Way when my friend Tom attempted to run an FKT (fastest known time) of this 173-kilometre route a few years ago and brought a group of us together to help crew him. I ended up with the graveyard shift, helping guide a very tired Tom (which was good, really, as it was the only time I could keep up with him) through 19 kilometres of Dartmoor trails, singing Miley Cyrus to keep his spirits up and startling more than a few sheep along the way.

Of course, this perhaps wasn't the best way to see Dartmoor given that it was pitch black at the time, but several trips back since make me feel confident in recommending it. The main reason I'm including it here is that the Two Moors Way offers a great way to explore some of the less public-transport-friendly parts of the moor, as your legs do the job of the bus. It makes for an excellent through-hike, if you (wisely) don't fancy tackling it all in one go like Tom.

So where exactly do those 173 kilometres take you? The Two Moors Way is a coast-to-coast trail across the breadth of Devon, starting in Wembury on the south coast and finishing in Lynmouth in the north. You don't just get to enjoy Dartmoor either – you also get to explore the equally brilliant Exmoor and the mid-Devon countryside sandwiched between the two moors. I honestly think that these two magnificent moors offer some of the most stunning scenery in the south of England, from Dartmoor's heather, hills and distinctive tors to Exmoor's steep valleys, woodland and wildlife. Plus there are ponies everywhere.

The official website for the Two Moors Way splits it into 13 sections, which vary quite a lot in distance (the shortest being 6 kilometres and the longest 26 kilometres) due to starting and finishing in villages with accommodation options and amenities. You can add some extra flexibility into your adventure by choosing to camp. For a shorter trip, have a go at just the Dartmoor section. The easiest way to do this would be to start in Ivybridge (which has a railway station) and finish just past Drewsteignton where you can pick up a bus to Okehampton, giving you around 60 kilometres to cover.

> **If you liked this**
> If you want to see more of Dartmoor, take the train to Ivybridge in the south and use that as your jumping-off point. For something different, try exploring Devon's other moor, Exmoor. Take the train to Barnstaple and the bus on to Lynmouth for both spectacular coastline and rugged inland walks. The Exmoor Coaster bus will help you get around once you're there too, travelling all the way to Porlock on the north-eastern side of the national park.

ENGLAND & THE ISLES

Jurassic Coast

> **BASE LOCATION** Swanage
>
> **WHERE TO STAY** Wide range of B&Bs, hotels and self-catering accommodation in Swanage, plus YHA Swanage and plenty of campsites nearby. California Meadows (2km from the centre of Swanage) is a great back-to-basics campsite.
>
> **HOW TO GET THERE** Train to Wareham or Poole then bus to Swanage

The Jurassic Coast is England's first UNESCO Natural World Heritage Site. It stretches for 155 kilometres between Swanage and Exmouth, crossing the Dorset/Devon border as it goes. Whichever part you choose to explore, you'll find yourself immersed in 185 million years of history, visible in the rock formations you'll see along the way.

If you ask me what my favourite section of the British coast is, I'll probably tell you the Jurassic Coast, and if you ask me to specify further, I'll say the bit around the Purbeck peninsula in Dorset. Separated from Poole and Bournemouth by a narrow strip of sea, the Isle of Purbeck is bordered by water on three sides. Basing yourself in Swanage gives you the opportunity to explore the coast in several directions, while also heading inland on to some of the incredible trails sweeping over the Purbeck Hills. Swanage itself is a decent-sized town and can get extremely busy at peak times, but I visited during a sunny spell in the school holidays, and I didn't have to walk or run far to find some peace and quiet on the trails. And the advantage of Swanage's size means you've got plenty of amenities and accommodation options. If you're on a budget, check out YHA Swanage or one of the many campsites nearby.

This section is full of winding coast paths, historic ruins, secluded swimming spots and some truly fantastic pubs. My top piece of advice for any day out on the Purbeck peninsula is to factor in it taking at least twice as long as you expect, because if your willpower is anything like mine you *will* end up stopping for refreshments, whether that's a cold drink on a summer's day in one of Dorset's incredible pub gardens, or cosying up in front of a fire with a tankard of hot cider.

1 Overlooking Lulworth Cove © Becky the Traveller **2–3 South West Coast Path** **4 Broadstands Beach** © Becky the Traveller

1 Anvil Point Lighthouse © Ian Woolcock/Shutterstock.com   **2** Old Harry Rocks

11 Durlston Country Park and Anvil Point

CATEGORY **Short**   DISTANCE **6km**   ASCENT **150m**   START/FINISH **Swanage**
MORE INFORMATION **www.durlston.co.uk**

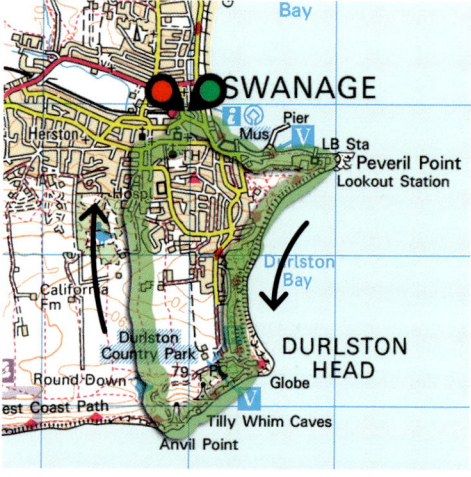

If you want to learn more about the landscape you're moving through, then Durlston Country Park is a great place to start. Covering the area of coast directly bordering the southern end of Swanage, this designated nature reserve is also home to a visitor centre which recently received a Visit England Gold Award for Accessible and Inclusive Tourism. Free to access, the centre is housed in a unique Victorian building and gives you a chance to learn more about the Jurassic Coast's history.

Durlston Country Park itself is teeming with wildlife. You can find a useful calendar on their website highlighting what you can expect to see each month, with migrating birds in the spring, wild flower meadows during the summer months and the chance to see bottlenose dolphins over the winter (if you're very lucky – remember to report any sightings on their website). Following this 6-kilometre loop from Swanage allows you to explore everything Durlston has to offer, along with seeing the lighthouse at Anvil Point. I'd also recommend straying off route and spending some time getting lost in the network of paths covering the country park.

12 Old Harry Rocks

| CATEGORY **Medium** | DISTANCE **13km** | ASCENT **230m** | START/FINISH **Swanage** |

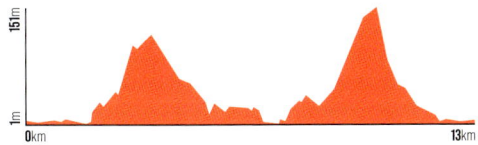

Old Harry Rocks are a series of chalk stacks which rise out of the sea at the southern end of Studland Bay, just to the north-east of Swanage, with the one furthest out to sea being Old Harry himself. If you've ever been to the Isle of Wight, you might be familiar with The Needles, another rock formation; thousands of years ago the two were actually linked by a series of chalk hills. These eroded away during the last ice age though, and today there's nothing but salt water between them.

This route skirts around the dramatic headland, giving you a good view of Old Harry and his neighbours from every angle, before heading into Studland village (where you can find several cafes, pubs and shops) and then over Ballard Down and back to Swanage. An advance warning to anybody who is as terrified of cows as I am: this area was teeming with them when I visited most recently, in early August. A man who passed me while I was standing paralysed with fear in a field, surrounded in all directions, assured me they were friendly, and I have to admit he seemed to be right. But still, don't say I didn't warn you! I also realise that some of you might actually *enjoy* meeting some nice, friendly cows. In which case, fill your boots.

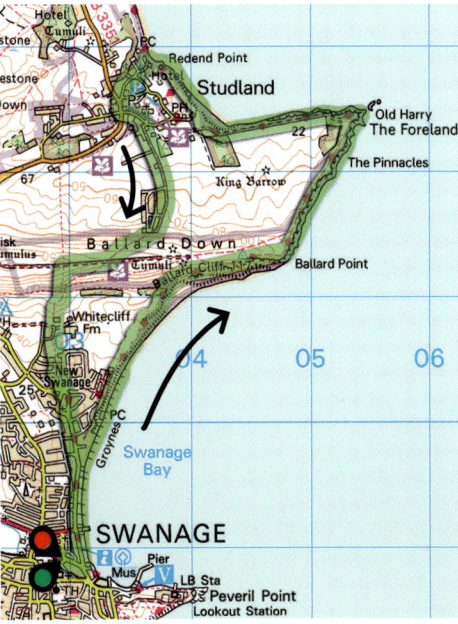

1 Dancing Ledge © Corbin Adler/Shutterstock.com

13 Worth Matravers and the Priest's Way

CATEGORY **Long**   DISTANCE **18km**
ASCENT **310m**   START/FINISH **Swanage**

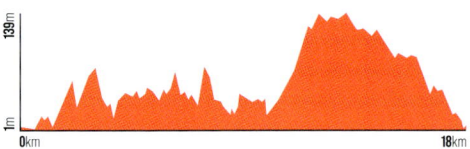

The 9 kilometres of coast path between Swanage and Winspit Quarry are some of my favourite in the country. Following the high clifftops, you can expect to see cliffs jutting dramatically out to sea and water that at times looks astoundingly bright turquoise. You'll go around Durlston Head and past Dancing Ledge, a shelf of rock housing a natural sea pool which is the perfect spot for a dip to cool off on a hot day.

The first time I tried to do this route was very much not a hot day though, and with severe weather warnings out and dangerously high winds, I opted to take a more inland route and follow the Priest's Way. It's a fairly straightforward track, with the main source of interest being that you get to follow in the footsteps of a medieval priest. But following it on a winter's day several years ago put me in the right place at the right time to meet the man who directed me to what is now my favourite pub in the world. We stopped to chat after he apologised for his dog barking at me and he told me in no uncertain terms that, whatever I did, I *had* to stop at the Square and Compass in Worth Matravers.

I was in a bit of a hurry and didn't really fancy a pub stop, but for some reason I took his advice. I'm so glad I did as, half an hour later, I was sitting in front of an open fire, eating a pasty (the only savoury thing on the menu), followed by Dorset apple cake for pudding, with a tankard of hot cider in my hand. On a sunny day, you can sit out at the front and enjoy views out to the sea; make sure you poke your head into the adjoining fossil museum too. It turns out the Square and Compass is Dorset's most famous pub and not the hidden gem I'd hoped it was (and even less so now I've written about it in this book) but it's still worth a visit. This route takes you out along the coast path – the longer leg – then back along the Priest's Way, after you've stopped at the pub.

WALK BRITAIN

1–2 Corfe Castle 3 South West Coast Path

14 Corfe Castle

CATEGORY **Challenge**   DISTANCE **29km**
ASCENT **540m**   START/FINISH **Swanage**

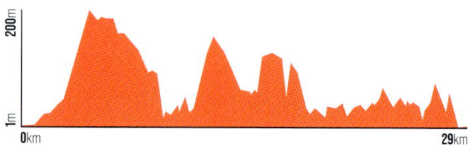

It's a bold claim and perhaps I shouldn't have favourites, but I think this might be one of the best routes in this book. Early on you have a slightly dull kilometre or so on the road to get you out of Swanage but after that it's 'all killer, no filler'. Get ready for an absolutely dreamy cocktail of coast paths, inland trails, ice cream stops, historic ruins, 'friendly' cows, pub gardens and secret coves.

You'll spend the first part of the day inland, following the Purbeck Way – this trail allows you to really see why this area has been awarded National Landscape status. Travelling over the spine of the Purbeck Ridgeway you're treated to views of the sea on either side and, if you turn to face east, you'll see it in three directions as it hugs the peninsula. It's perhaps a little early in the day at this point for a picnic, but there are plenty of mounds along the way to stop and enjoy the view from.

For me the highlight is the approach to Corfe Castle. The village is named after the ruins which stand above it, the last remains of William the Conqueror's castle which was apparently one of the earliest to be built with stone in England. Standing atop the hill, overlooking the village, this landmark is visible from all around. (For the ultimate 'room with a view', take the bus or a steam train on the Swanage Railway from Swanage to Harman's Cross and stay at Downshay Farm campsite.

If you pitch your tent right, you'll get to watch the sun setting over the castle in the distance.)

Walking along the ridge towards the castle, the imposing ruins grow closer with every step. For me, with the sun shining, it was one of those moments that make up for all the other days I've spent battling storms and trudging through clouds. It seemed like everybody else out on the trails felt the same too – my progress was significantly slowed by saying hello to a dog and their owner approximately every 150 metres. I was even in too good a mood to pay attention to the cows hanging out in the field on the final approach to the village. It must have been a good day!

For a shorter option, you can take the bus or train back to Swanage from Corfe Castle. If you're carrying on, after stopping for a light mid-walk snack of a giant pasty (optional but recommended from the Corfe Castle Village Bakery), it's time to head back towards the coast. Following the Hardy Way for a few kilometres you pass through Kingston, where you can stop at the Scott Arms if you fancy a break with a view in their impressive garden. Picking up the coast path for the final stretch back to Swanage, there are some steep hills to tackle and at times seemingly endless steps up to scale them. Luckily, you've got the stunning sea views to distract you, along with plenty of opportunities to scramble down to the sea for a dip. Keep an eye out for Chapman's Pool, a remote cove which generally remains quiet even at peak times due to the effort required to reach it.

From Winspit Quarry, you follow the same stretch of coast path as in route 13 but in the opposite direction. It's a fantastic bit of coastline, so who wouldn't want to walk it twice!

1 Jurassic Coast Path 2 Looking back on the trail
3 Hiking towards Durdle Door All photos © Becky the Traveller

15 Jurassic Coast Path

> CATEGORY **Multi-day** DISTANCE **189km** ASCENT **3,410m** START **Studland Heath** FINISH **Exmouth**
> PUBLIC TRANSPORT **Outbound: train to Poole, then bus to Sandbanks, then take the chain ferry to Studland Heath. Return: train from Exmouth.** MORE INFORMATION www.southwestcoastpath.org.uk

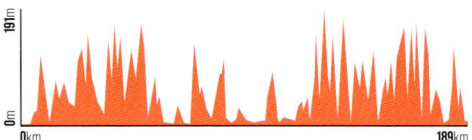

The Jurassic Coast acts as either the opening or closing chapter of the South West Coast Path, depending on which direction you tackle the 1,000-kilometre-long trail, but it makes for a fantastic standalone adventure too. Most people will take six or seven days over it, but as always you can split it up however you like. Climb South West run a number of events on the Jurassic Coast Path including the Jurassic Extinction 105-mile ultra, if you're in the market for a (very big) challenge.

Over the Jurassic Coast's 189 kilometres, you get to experience some of the most diverse terrain of the whole South West Coast Path, despite only covering a fraction of its length.

As well as roller-coaster clifftop trails and endless beaches to explore, you'll also visit Undercliffs National Nature Reserve, England's answer to a tropical rainforest.

After arriving in Poole, you take the ferry over to Studland Bay from Sandbanks (which you probably don't want to take too much of a liking to, as it's the UK's most expensive seaside town to buy a house in) and then spend some time exploring the areas already covered in this section. From there it's all fresh trail and over the course of your adventure you'll pass sights including Durdle Door, probably the subject of more photographs than anywhere else in Dorset, and Chesil Beach, made famous by Ian McEwan's novel. Despite the solitude of the trails, the popularity of the South Coast means you'll find plenty of amenities on route and even luggage transfer services (*luggagetransfers.co.uk*).

> **If you liked this**
> The Jurassic Coast continues on all the way to Exmouth and you'll do worse than to move your attention westwards and continue exploring along it. As well as the coast, there's also a huge area of inland Dorset that sits within the National Landscape boundary and is definitely worth visiting. Look at the full Hardy Way route for some inspiration – you can easily take the train to Dorchester and pick it up there.

ENGLAND & THE ISLES

London Day Trips

> BASE LOCATION **Anywhere in London**
>
> WHERE TO STAY **London has a huge variety of accommodation – from hostels to high-end hotels**
>
> HOW TO GET THERE **Rail connections to Central London, then use the Underground or Overgound to travel around**

A city of 9 million people might not be the most obvious choice for an adventure hub but it's hard to beat London for the sheer number of fantastic outdoor locations which are within easy reach. Take a quick glance at the map and you'll see that the capital is surrounded by areas of green space, many of which are just a short train ride away. This chapter gives you a few options for different day trips, all around an hour's journey from a London station. Perfect for when your annual leave is running low but you still want to escape the smog and breathe in some fresh(er) air.

These are the places I used to disappear to on a Sunday when I still lived in London, setting off first thing on a blissfully quiet train and returning covered in mud on a late afternoon train, ready for work on a Monday morning. Over the following pages you'll visit multiple National Landscapes and have the chance to wander through a whole variety of scenery, from atmospheric woodlands and rolling farmland to invigorating coast paths and well-kept parks. The one thing they all have in common is that their beauty belies the concrete jungle that at times is less than 10 kilometres away as the crow flies.

I've chosen my favourite route in each location but I'm sure it goes without saying that there are plenty more for you to discover, giving you ample opportunity for many more day trips in the future. Most of these would make for a good one-night break too, when you want to minimise your travel time and maximise your trail time.

1 Hikers in Epping Forest near Chingford © Epping Forest Heritage Trust **2** Beautiful thatched cottage near Westcott, Surrey Hills © Jane Beagley **3** Blatchford Down, Surrey Hills © Jane Beagley **4** Leith Hill Tower, Surrey Hills © Jane Beagley **5** Hikers in Epping Forest near High Beach © Epping Forest Heritage Trust **6** Woodland near Leith Hill, Surrey Hills © Jane Beagley

16 Epping Forest

CATEGORY **Medium**	DISTANCE **12km**	ASCENT **140m**	START **Chingford**	FINISH **Theydon Bois**

PUBLIC TRANSPORT **Outbound: London Overground services from London Liverpool Street to Chingford (25 minutes). Return: Central Line from Theydon Bois (50 minutes).** MORE INFORMATION www.efht.org.uk

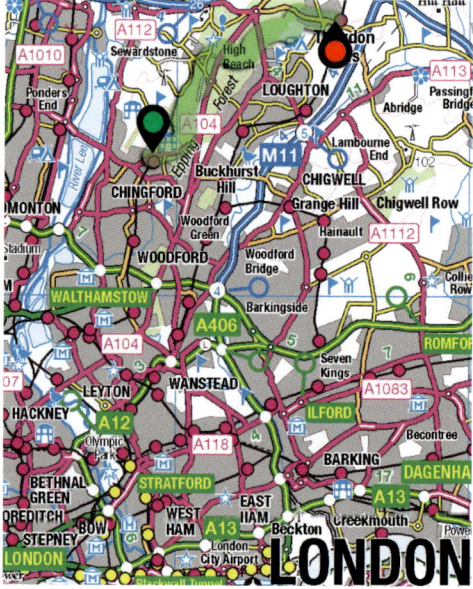

I lived on the edge of Epping Forest for the best part of a year, and it felt like the best of both worlds. Miles and miles of incredible trails on my doorstep in one direction, a choice of ten great places to go for brunch and the Victoria Line in the other. I only had to run for ten minutes and the city felt totally left behind (except for the gentle hum of the North Circular which I could occasionally hear in the background …).

The Epping Forest Big Walk (previously known as the Centenary Walk) is a 24-kilometre trail that runs through the entire length of the forest but I think that this 12-kilometre stretch takes in the best parts of it. Starting from Chingford station, you only have to walk a few hundred metres before you're in the forest and beginning your journey through its tree-lined trails. I've included a little detour to Connaught Water, which is a great place to see a good mix of birds up close (just don't feed them). The herons look particularly serene if you catch one perched by the water's edge.

Birdwatching over you'll join back up with the main route. It's mostly a wide path so suitable for pushchairs and wheelchairs but there are also lots of little trails into the trees that you can venture on to if you're feeling a little more intrepid. As you approach Theydon Bois station and the end of your walk, you'll skirt around the deer sanctuary.

There's no public access to the sanctuary but you can often see deer as you walk past, especially if you bring binoculars. The history of deer in Epping Forest is actually really interesting and a topic Ken Hoy covers well in his book, *Getting to Know Epping Forest*.

The forest is beautiful at all times of the year: luscious and green in the summer, a kaleidoscope of warm-toned leaves in the autumn, stark and enchanting on a frosty winter's day and wonderfully hopeful as everything starts to come to life again in the spring. If you fancy tackling the whole of the Epping Forest Big Walk, the Epping Forest Heritage Trust organises a free group walk of the trail every September.

17 Chilterns

CATEGORY **Medium**   DISTANCE **14km**   ASCENT **250m**   START/FINISH **Tring**   PUBLIC TRANSPORT **Both ways: trains between London Euston and Tring (40 minutes)**

Tring is one of the stops on the railway between Northampton, where I grew up, and London. I must have travelled through it hundreds of times, figuring it was just another commuter town, before it occurred to me that it was a place I might want to visit. When I did eventually get off the train at Tring and went for my first hike around the Chiltern Hills, I couldn't believe that somewhere this nice existed along the route of my daily commute.

The Chilterns National Landscape covers part of the chalk escarpment which crosses England all the way from Yorkshire to Dorset. An escarpment basically just means a steep slope and their dramatic nature not only makes them great to look at, but also means they form an important habitat for many rare species. You'll see one excellent example of this early on in the day as you head through Aldbury Nowers Nature Reserve, which is one of the best places in the country to see wild flowers, butterflies and even solitary bees. From the nature reserve you begin the steady climb up to Ivinghoe Beacon, which is actually the official start point of The Ridgeway trail. At 140 kilometres long and taking you all the way to Wiltshire, it's definitely one to look at for a longer adventure if you enjoy this kind of landscape. It certainly has a spectacular starting point – on a clear day you can see for miles from the top of Ivinghoe Beacon.

As well as the vast views you'll experience from the high points of this route, you'll also get to explore some of the woodland that the Chilterns are known for. Over half of the area's woodland is ancient and perhaps the highlight on this loop is the red cedar woods you'll find as you descend from the Beacon. One Komoot user wrote: 'If there is magic in the world it's here …' – I'm not sure I need to say much more! The woods make for an impressive contrast to the exposed trails you've just been walking on.

The route finishes back at Tring station but if you're hungry post-walk, it's another 2 kilometres into the town centre where you'll find lots of options. The Espresso Lounge has great coffee and pastries.

1 View from Ditchling Beacon © Melanie Hobson/Shutterstock.com   2 RSPB Cliffe Pools © Joyce Qian/Shutterstock.com

18 South Downs

CATEGORY **Medium**   DISTANCE **15km**
ASCENT **260m**   START **Falmer**   FINISH **Lewes**
PUBLIC TRANSPORT **Outbound: train to Falmer, via Brighton (1 hour 30 minutes). Return: train from Lewes, via Haywards Heath (1 hour 10 minutes).**

I spent a long time pondering which route in the South Downs to include as there are so many great spots, from the distinctive chalk cliffs of the Seven Sisters near Eastbourne to the iconic view over Devil's Dyke. In the end I decided on this A-to-B adventure from Falmer to Lewes taking in Ditchling Beacon, which is the highest point in East Sussex.

Falmer is home to the University of Sussex, and they certainly picked a beautiful spot for the campus. Leaving the station behind you'll first walk through the wooded edge of Stanmer Park on your way to Ditchling Beacon. It's a popular spot with cyclists and not only do you get panoramic views from the top, but if you're lucky you'll also find an ice cream van waiting for you. This is a godsend on a warm day as some of the route is quite exposed (the trade-off for those expansive views). At Ditchling Beacon you pick up the South Downs Way, which you'll follow towards Lewes. It's a stunning ridge walk, especially as you head over Blackcap and Mount Harry.

It's worth spending some time in Lewes if you've never visited before. As well as being surrounded by the chalk hills you've just walked over, it's also got a thriving arts scene and is home to a brilliant selection of independent shops. Have a wander around the narrow medieval streets or take a trip up to the castle, which somewhat dominates the market town.

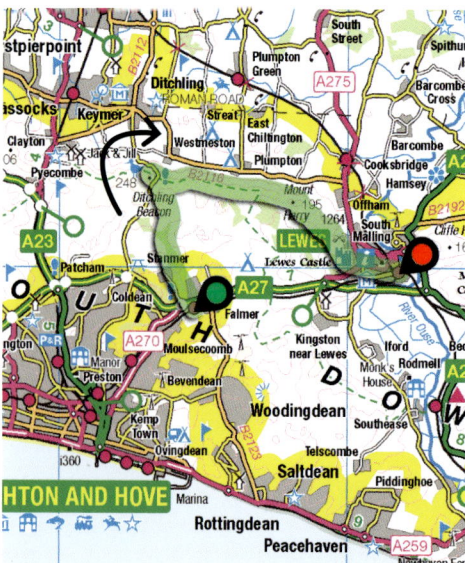

ENGLAND & THE ISLES

19 Hoo Peninsula

CATEGORY **Long** DISTANCE **23km** ASCENT **90m** START/FINISH **Cliffe, Hoo Peninsula** PUBLIC TRANSPORT **Both ways: buses between London and Strood (35 minutes) and buses between Strood and Cliffe (30 minutes)**

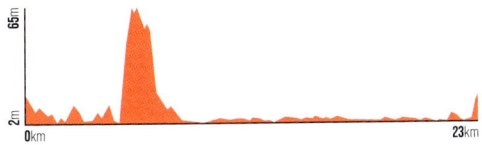

The Hoo Peninsula is a forgotten sort of place, sitting nestled in the Thames Estuary. It's a place you might have to work a little harder to love than some of the more obvious beauty spots I've included, but it's worth persevering with. Previously a key area for heavy industry, today nature has reclaimed this finger of land somewhat. Hoo is an important place for wildlife and home to two RSPB sites: Cliffe Pools and Northward Hill. This route takes in both of them, allowing you the special experience of sharing this important habitat that so many creatures call home.

You'll explore Northward Hill first which is a working farm, with grazing sheep and cows dotting the landscape and bluebell woods to enjoy in the spring. It occupies a ridge, giving you wide vistas over the otherwise flat Thames Marshes. It's hard to believe as you look around at the marshland that this whole area was drained in the 1940s, but the RSPB have worked hard to restore the wetlands. As well as a stunning array of bird species to be seen through your binoculars, this also means the area is popular with various wading creatures, from waterfowl to some incredibly rare invertebrates. My main advice for this walk is not to rush around it because there's so much to see once you start looking.

From Northward Hill you'll drop down and pick up one of the newly opened sections of the King Charles III England Coast Path, which will take you around to Cliffe Pools and then eventually back up to Cliffe to catch the bus again. Our full route is 23 kilometres, but you can easily divide it into segments for a shorter day out. The whole area is incredibly flat, so don't worry about any steep ground or hills. It can get muddy after wet spells though, so make sure you're wearing some good grippy footwear.

WALK BRITAIN

1 Albert's Coffee Bar in Gomshall 2 View from Leith Hill 3 Leith Hill Tower
4 North Downs Way woodland All photos © Jane Beagley

20 Surrey Hills

CATEGORY **Long**   DISTANCE **24km**   ASCENT **440m**   START/FINISH **Gomshall**   PUBLIC TRANSPORT **Both ways: trains between London Waterloo and Gomshall (change at Guildford or Redhill; 1 hour–1 hour 30 minutes)**

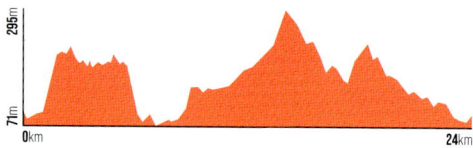

The Surrey Hills National Landscape covers more than a quarter of the county of Surrey and is littered with train stations, making it incredibly easy to get out into nature from London. There are some fantastic footpaths around the area, the best of which will take you through a hefty mix of open commons, high viewpoints and enclosed woodland. For all these reasons, this is an incredibly popular area with walkers, runners and cyclists but you should still be able to find some pockets of peace and quiet. This circular route starts from Gomshall and takes in a combination of the Surrey Hills' most famous viewpoints along with some hidden gems. For a pre-walk energy boost, check out Albert's Coffee Bar in Gomshall, an open-air cafe that gets top marks for their selection of hot drinks and cakes.

The walk itself first crosses the railway and picks up the North Downs Way for a while, then runs through Blatchford Down (where the day's good views begin) and past several World War II pill boxes. Heading south, you'll cross the railway again before making your way through some lovely woodland. Look out for Tillingbourne Waterfall – this natural cascade is somewhat of a 'secret' spot. From here the climb up to Leith Hill begins. Leath Hill Tower is the highest point in South East England; on a clear day you can reportedly see 13 counties from the top! Not a feat I've ever managed, but attempting to count them could be a fun challenge if visibility is good.

The popularity of this route means I sadly can't promise you the same sense of remoteness you'll find elsewhere. However, the trade-off for this is a steady stream of snack stops you'll pass along the way. Having already caffeinated up in Gomshall, you'll also find a cafe at Leith Hill Tower and a coffee bar in a barn as you cross over towards Hurtwood Common (Heartwork Coffee Bar). At 24 kilometres this is a fairly long walk, but I can promise you won't go hungry.

If you liked this
As well as there being many more routes in the places I've mentioned in this chapter, there are also several more green spaces close to London that I've not been able to include. Check out the Kent Downs, High Weald and the North Wessex Downs, all of which are designated National Landscapes. There are lots of trails to explore within London too, including those at Richmond Park and Hampstead Heath. Then there are long-distance trails, such as the Thames Path, the Capital Ring or the Jubilee Greenway – you can tackle them in one go for a big adventure or work your way through in segments.

ENGLAND & THE ISLES

Norfolk Broads

> BASE LOCATION **Great Yarmouth**
>
> WHERE TO STAY **Wide range of B&Bs, hotels and self-catering accommodation in Great Yarmouth, including budget accommodation. Closest campsite is Vauxhall Holiday Park (1km from Great Yarmouth station).**
>
> HOW TO GET THERE **Trains to Great Yarmouth from Norwich**

The Norfolk Broads are a little different compared to the other areas I've written about so far. While most of the routes I've included involve marvelling over various natural wonders, the Broads are actually a man-made landscape. Their tapestry of waterways is the result of intensive medieval peat digging, as revealed by the botanist Dr Joyce Lambert in the 1950s. The business of peat extraction came to an end when the area was flooded in the 14th century, creating lakes which eventually joined up with local rivers and formed the Broads as we know them today, the UK's only man-made national park.

Peat digging was a difficult job so I feel fairly assured in promising you that wandering around the Norfolk Broads will be a much more pleasant experience. I think I can also safely say that this is the flattest chapter, with only 330 metres of climbing over the entire 133 kilometres covered in the following routes. But what the area lacks in high viewpoints it more than makes up for with almost unfathomably wide skies and a wealth of wildlife; the Broads is the UK's largest protected wetland. The Norfolk Broads are home to over 25 per cent of the rare species in the UK and I've tried to give you the opportunity to see as many of them as possible.

Great Yarmouth is our base for this section. While perhaps not the most quaint of places, it's ideal for accessing other areas of the national park, with the train line towards Norwich allowing you to explore inland and a coastal bus service to take you north. Great Yarmouth is also somewhat a miracle. Where it stands was once part of a vast estuary, with no solid ground to speak of. Over time the estuary was filled in by a bank of sand and shingle which collected at its mouth, which eventually dried out to form the land on which the town stands.

If you're content exploring more locally then you could choose to base yourself around one of the routes instead. The pretty village of Winterton-on-Sea makes for a good seaside option, or Reedham if you'd prefer to stay inland.

1 Berney Arms Mill from Burgh Castle   **2** Roman walls of Gariannonum Fort   **3** Angles Way signpost at Burgh Castle
4 Stone's Drainage Mill   **5** Red Mill across the River Waveney   **6** St Andrew's Church, Wickhampton   All photos © Joe Jackson

41

WALK BRITAIN

1 Seal on the Norfolk Coast © Paul Maguire/Shutterstock.com

21 Winterton Circular

CATEGORY **Short** DISTANCE **8km** ASCENT **20m** START/FINISH **Winterton-on-Sea**
PUBLIC TRANSPORT **Both ways: buses between Great Yarmouth and Winterton-on-Sea (35 minutes)**

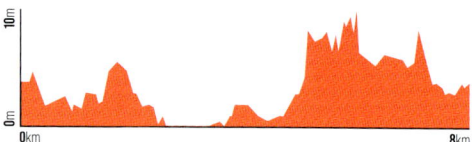

The coastal village of Winterton-on-Sea, around 13 kilometres north of Great Yarmouth, is probably best known for its beaches. It's not just the acres of soft, golden sand that this stretch of coast has to boast about though, but also the fact that Winterton shares its beaches with a colony of seals. Home to both grey and common seals, you've got a good chance of spotting them at any time of year but it's during the winter that the beach really comes alive, with hundreds of white-furred pups being born. It's an incredible sight but make sure you don't get too close – these pups may look cute and fluffy, but you'll find yourself facing the wrath of their mother should you try to pet them. They're best enjoyed from a safe distance with a pair of binoculars.

As well as giving you ample seal-spotting opportunities, this 8-kilometre circular walk also takes you inland to explore some of the marshes which make up the Winterton Dunes National Nature Reserve. Another highlight is the ivy-clad ruins of St Mary's Church, which was abandoned in the 17th century and is today largely hidden by the nature growing around it. Find your way in and stand at the base of the oak tree which rises from the centre of the ruins, whose height will give you a sense of just how long it has stood for. Make sure you keep an eye out for any falling oak leaves too, as legend goes that catching one will bring you good luck and prosperity. My dad is convinced that this is true, as he reportedly caught a leaf and then immediately found a £20 note on the floor.

If you're not quite ready to leave the beach behind at the end of the walk, stop off at Seal View Cafe for tasty snacks and hot drinks with an unrivalled view of the colony. Or for a longer walk, just keep heading north from Winterton Ness before turning and returning back to Winterton.

ENGLAND & THE ISLES

22 Berney Marshes

> CATEGORY **Medium**   DISTANCE **16km**   ASCENT **20m**   START/FINISH **Berney Arms station**
> PUBLIC TRANSPORT **Both ways: trains between Great Yarmouth and Berney Arms (10 minutes). This is a request-only stop so make sure you let the conductor know where you're going. There are only a couple of services a day, so make sure you check timings before travel.**

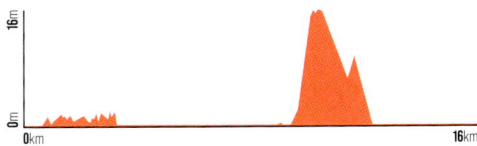

Berney Arms station sits on an offshoot of the line between Norwich and Great Yarmouth. It's a request-only stop and was recently named Britain's least used railway station after seeing just 42 passengers in a whole year between 2019 and 2020. Use it or lose it though and this claim to fame actually caused a surge of visitors, with an impressive 348 people using the station the following year. Yep, still less than one per day.

Clearly this is a good place to head if you want to avoid the crowds. Something that makes Berney Arms an even more perfect starting point for a car-free adventure is the fact that there's actually no road access to the station at all; you can only reach it by boat or on foot. We'll be going for the latter mode of transport with this 16-kilometre walk around the marshes which surround the station.

Berney Marshes nature reserve is the place to come if you want to experience the wide skies and grazing marshes for which the Norfolk Broads are known. It's a fantastic walk all year round, traversing the edge of Breydon Water estuary and roaming around reed-bordered tracks. Visiting in the spring you'll get to see the impressive display of lapwings and redshanks courting, while in the winter large flocks of various birds gather here, including golden plover and wigeon. Something else to look out for is Berney Arms Windmill, one of Norfolk's largest marsh mills which was in use until 1948. At the time of writing it's closed to visitors for maintenance, but it's an imposing structure which still makes for an impressive sight looming above the flat landscape.

Unfortunately, the Berney Arms pub, after which the station is named, has been closed for several years. There aren't any other spots to get refreshments on this route so make sure you bring a picnic.

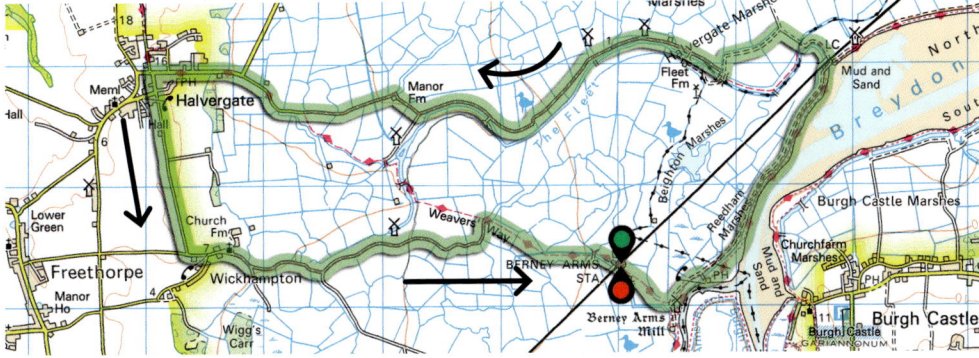

WALK BRITAIN

1 Grazing Marsh near Acle   2 Berney Marshes Both photos © Joe Jackson

23 Acle to Great Yarmouth

CATEGORY **Long**   DISTANCE **19km**   ASCENT **30m**
START **Acle**   FINISH **Great Yarmouth**   PUBLIC TRANSPORT **Outbound: train or bus from Great Yarmouth to Acle (15 minutes)**

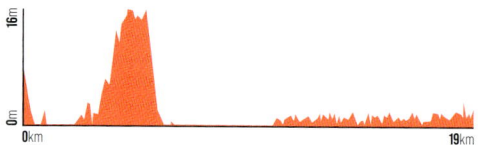

In its entirety, the Weavers' Way is 98 kilometres long and will take you all the way from Cromer to Great Yarmouth, essentially linking the north and east coasts of Norfolk. Named for the weaving industry which flourished in the area during the Middle Ages, this final stretch of the Way begins in Acle and finishes in Great Yarmouth.

Setting off from Acle station, you'll make your way across Halvergate Marshes first, passing through Halvergate village along the way (which has a pub, complete with a very popular pub dog, if you're looking for lunch). For some further reading, there's actually a book available to buy online entitled: *It Happens in Halvergate: A pretty crap tourist guide to a small village in Norfolk*. Writer Laurence Hinton describes the landscape which surrounds Halvergate as 'Acres and acres of flat dull grassland'. However, one person's trash is another's treasure, because this isn't just grass; it's a teeming habitat for the literally hundreds of species which call it home. From the birds I mentioned in route 22 (you'll visit Berney Marshes on this route too) to a large range of freshwater plants and invertebrates, it's worth bringing your binoculars along for this walk.

The final portion of the route skirts around the entire northern shore of Breydon Water before finishing in Great Yarmouth, where a fitting way to end the day is with fish and chips on the beach. There are plenty of indoor eating options for bad-weather days too – Great Yarmouth has something of a burgeoning food scene.

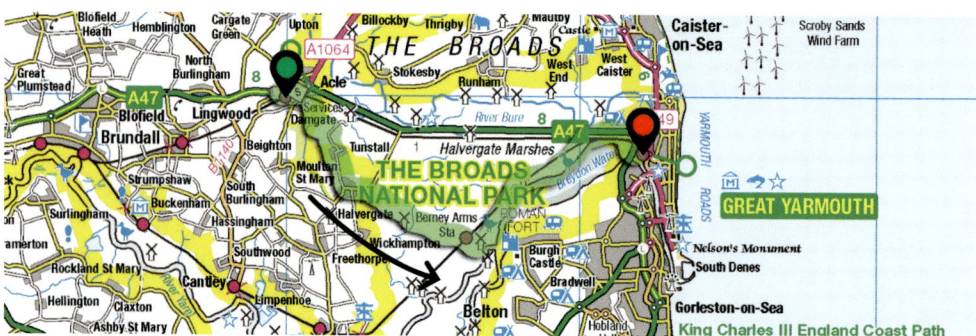

44

ENGLAND & THE ISLES

24 Great Yarmouth to Oulton Broad

CATEGORY **Challenge** DISTANCE **30km**
ASCENT **100m** START **Great Yarmouth**
FINISH **Oulton Broad** PUBLIC TRANSPORT **Return: train from Oulton Broad to Great Yarmouth, via Brundall (1 hour 30 minutes)**

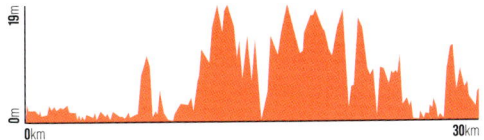

This route offers the opportunity to explore the southern Broads, walking from Great Yarmouth south to Oulton Broad. You'll be following the Angles Way, a long-distance trail that some consider to be one of the best waterside routes in the country. This section will take you around Breydon Water, then on to Burgh Castle which was built as a Roman defence way back in the 3rd century. Three of its walls are standing to nearly their full original height, making it not only one of the best-preserved Roman monuments you'll find in Britain, but also an interesting contrast to the surrounding flat marshland of the Broads.

You leave the water after Burgh Castle and spend the rest of the day peacefully ambling through the type of quiet countryside that Norfolk does incredibly well. The route finishes at Oulton Broad, considered to be the southern gateway to the Broads. From here you can catch a train back into Great Yarmouth but if you've got some time to spare first, the Commodore has a great beer garden overlooking the water. For a shorter walk, stop in Somerleyton (22 kilometres into the walk) and hop on the train there instead.

45

1 Norton Drainage Mill **2** Wherryman's Way signpost near Whitlingham
3 Rockland Broad **4** Rockland Staithe All photos © Joe Jackson

25 Wherryman's Way

CATEGORY **Multi-day** DISTANCE **60km** ASCENT **160m** START **Norwich** FINISH **Great Yarmouth**
PUBLIC TRANSPORT **Outbound: train to Norwich. Return: train from Great Yarmouth.**

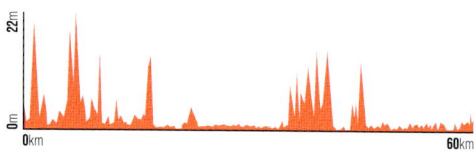

At 60 kilometres long, the Wherryman's Way is the perfect length for a long weekend adventure. The marked riverside route links Norwich with Great Yarmouth, giving you easy public transport access at either end. It's one of only two ways you can really experience the River Yare, which you'll follow for the majority of your time, the other being by boat. Fittingly, the trail is named after the men who operated 'wherries', large barges which were traditionally used to transport both cargo and passengers around the east of England before cars took over.

As you travel through this large swathe of the Broads, you'll visit some of the places I've mentioned in this section already, including Berney Arms Windmill and Berney Marshes, but with many new sights alongside them. Perhaps one of the most interesting things about the Wherryman's Way is the unique waymarkers you'll find along the way. Forget your bog-standard signposts; instead you'll be guided by a range of statues, from steel wherry sails to life-size figures.

My favourite of these waymarkers is the one near Bramerton depicting 'Billy Bluelight'. Born in a slum in Norwich in 1859, Billy became somewhat of a cult figure by making a living racing pleasure boats along a 30-kilometre stretch of the River Yare. Billy would run on the riverbanks alongside the boats and collect tips at the end from his adoring fans. In the summer, you'll still find plenty of boats out on the Yare to race if you so choose (I can't guarantee any success). Winter might be the best time to explore the Wherryman's Way though, when for the most part you'll likely share it only with the birds.

If you liked this
I've focused mostly on the inland areas of the Broads in this chapter but the whole Norfolk Coast is beautiful and has some great walking. The Norfolk Coast Path is 135 kilometres long and is one of Britain's official National Trails (in conjunction with the Peddars Way). For more wetlands, check out the Hoo Peninsula in Kent (route 19) or at the other end of the country try Caerlaverock National Nature Reserve (travel by train to Dumfries then bus to Caerlaverock).

ENGLAND & THE ISLES

Peak District

> BASE LOCATION **Anywhere on the Hope Valley railway line will give you easy access to all the routes in this section**
>
> WHERE TO STAY **Good range of self-catering accommodation and B&Bs in Edale, Hathersage, Hope and Bamford. YHAs in Hathersage and Edale. Multiple campsites in Edale close to the station.**
>
> HOW TO GET THERE **Train to Manchester or Sheffield then train to villages along the Hope Valley railway line**

My dad didn't start walking (in the recreational sense) until he was in his thirties. He had apparently 'heard about this thing called hillwalking', thought it sounded fun, bought himself a copy of *Trail* magazine and chose a route within day trip distance of where he lived in Northamptonshire. This happened to be in the Peak District and off he went for his first walk. Discovering he quite enjoyed it, but was often limited by having to look after me, this was also the point that my hillwalking career began. I was about six at the time and from this point onwards almost all of my childhood memories involve being reluctantly dragged up various hills, moaning a lot.

We carried on visiting the Peak District most frequently and if you'd asked me back then, I'm sure I would have been unable to fathom that there could possibly be a mountain bigger than Mam Tor. I've since learned that Mam Tor doesn't even officially qualify as a mountain (at 517 metres it's around 100 metres too short), but bigger isn't always better, and I still absolutely love visiting the Peak. Hopefully I don't moan at my dad *quite* as much these days, although I stand by the fact his snack selection in 1998 wasn't up to scratch.

I think that the Hope Valley railway line is one of the best resources we have here in Great Britain when it comes to a public-transport-friendly adventure. Connecting Manchester in the west and Sheffield in the east, the train line has stops dotted across the entire breadth of the Peak District National Park. The routes in this chapter allow you to explore a range of places along the line, ticking off key Peak District sights, from the giant mountain of Mam Tor (if six-year-old-me was writing this book) to the impressive Ladybower Reservoir and iconic gritstone edges.

1 Ladybower Reservoir © Jon Barton   **2** Edale Skyline © Jon Barton   **3** Peak District trails
4 Stanage Edge   **5** Edale Skyline © Sarah Lister

WALK BRITAIN

1 Ladybower Reservoir © Jon Barton   2 Mam Tor at sunrise

26 Ladybower Reservoir

CATEGORY **Short**   DISTANCE **7km**   ASCENT **120m**   START/FINISH **Bamford station**
PUBLIC TRANSPORT **Both ways: train to/from Bamford, if needed**

Ladybower is one of three large, linked reservoirs in the Upper Derwent Valley. Created by building huge dams (massive operations that took many years and thousands of workers to complete), these reservoirs are impressive feats of engineering and are worth a visit.

This circular walk from Bamford takes you up to Ladybower Reservoir and gives you an opportunity to cross the great dam. You'll follow the well-maintained Thornhill Trail on the way out, then a mixture of footpaths and country lanes on the way back. Although generally on good tracks and relatively flat, there are a few stiles on this route. For a more accessible option, you can walk along the road from Bamford up to the reservoir and then explore the dam using the designated Miles without Stiles route.

Stop in at the Yorkshire Bridge Inn for refreshments en route, including large portions of pub classics and slabs of Bakewell pudding. Back in Bamford, check out the community-owned Anglers Rest, a pub, cafe and post office all in one.

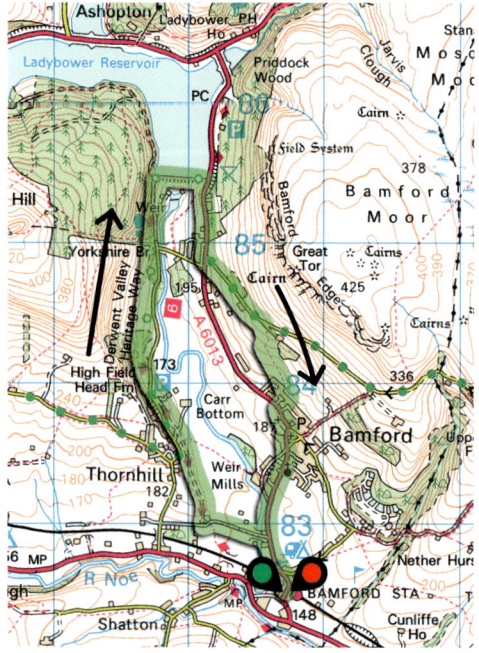

1

27 Mam Tor

CATEGORY **Medium**   DISTANCE **10km**   ASCENT **380m**   START/FINISH **Edale station**
PUBLIC TRANSPORT **Both ways: train to/from Edale, if needed**

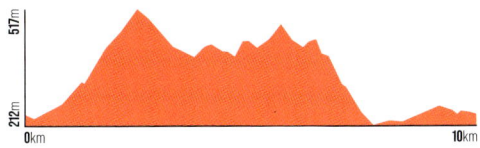

Mam Tor might not quite qualify as a mountain, but it still packs a punch in terms of effort-to-reward. The Great Ridge is an iconic section of trail, allowing you an experience often reserved for high mountain ridges. This one makes for a really great trail run – the perfect taster if you're thinking about having a go at the Edale Skyline at some point (route 29).

Heading out of Edale, which is a great base with its campsites, pubs and youth hostel, you'll climb up to Mam Tor first. That's the bulk of the hard work done, and from here you get to enjoy some truly fantastic ridge walking as you head along to Hollins Cross, Back Tor and Lose Hill, before turning back on yourself for a stretch (double the fun?) and then dropping back down to Edale. If the forecast is good, I can highly recommend setting an early alarm and getting yourself up here for sunrise. Not only will you hopefully get to witness a pretty spectacular panorama but it's also a way to avoid the inevitable crowds (unsurprisingly given everything I've just said, this is a *very* popular spot).

28 Stanage and Burbage Edges

CATEGORY **Medium** DISTANCE **15km**
ASCENT **370m** START/FINISH **Hathersage**
PUBLIC TRANSPORT **Both ways: train to/from Hathersage, if needed**

One of the things that the Peak District is best known for is its famous edges. These imposing gritstone crags were formed around 300 million years ago, caused by changing sea levels. The edges are divided into several sections but together make up a 20-kilometre-long wall of rock. They make the perfect playground for outdoors lovers, whether you're a climber taking advantage of the many routes and boulder problems, or a runner or hiker exploring the tops. In this route, you'll get to see two of the most popular sections: Stanage Edge and Burbage Edge.

If you're in need of a packed lunch pop to Hathersage Bakery before your walk for a well-priced and generously sized sandwich. From Hathersage you'll first head through some woodland before making your way up to Carl Wark, which gives you some excellent views over the Burbage Valley. In the summer, you'll see distinctive purple heather carpeting the landscape all around. From here, you make your way up on to your first edge of the day, Burbage, which will soon merge into Stanage Edge.

The main thing that has always struck me about Stanage Edge is how dramatic the landscape feels for a relatively gentle walk. It's the kind of visual pay-off normally reserved for routes with many times more metres of climbing. The path is rocky with steep edges though (as it says on the tin, I suppose) so take care while you enjoy the views. If you look carefully, you'll even see the small bullet holes in the rock which serve as a reminder of this area having been a training ground for soldiers during World War II.

Dropping down from the edge, you'll pass the remains of the medieval North Lees Chapel and then follow farm tracks back to Hathersage. There are lots of places to refuel in Hathersage – I love Colemans Deli in the daytime or Maazi in the evening, which is an almost surprisingly good Indian. If you're looking to cool off on a hot day, walk down the road a little way to Leadmill Bridge and then pick up the river path and you'll find various spots to paddle in the River Derwent. Or for a proper swim, Hathersage Swimming Pool is open air and heated all your round.

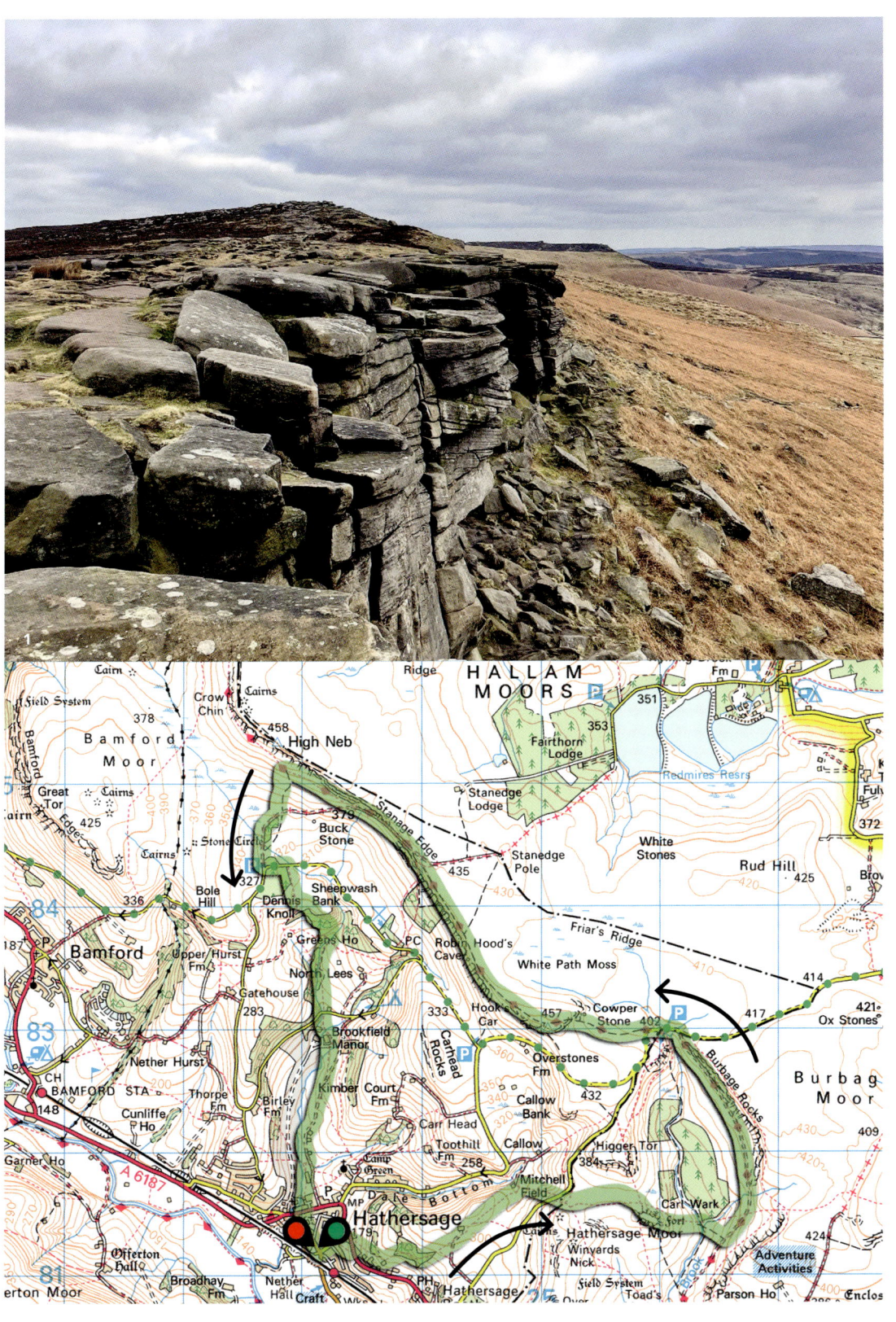

WALK BRITAIN

1 Edale Skyline © Jon Barton 2 Jaggers Clough 3 Win Hill

29 Edale Skyline

CATEGORY **Challenge** DISTANCE **33km**
ASCENT **830m** START/FINISH **Hope station**
PUBLIC TRANSPORT **Both ways: train to/from Hope, if needed**

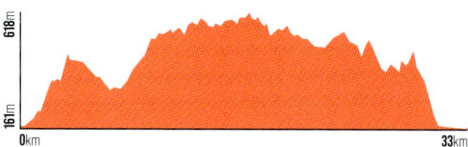

The Edale Skyline is a firm classic in terms of Peak District routes. It's a challenging day out at over 30 kilometres long and with more than 800 metres of ascent to tackle, but for me it ticks all the boxes for a fantastic long-distance route. It's circular with an easily accessible start and finish point at Hope station and offers an excellent variety of terrain and scenery.

It doesn't really matter which way around you approach this one, but I think anticlockwise works best. It means you tick Win Hill off first, rather than facing a climb down and back up at the end, which can feel a little demoralising on tired legs. Depending on what your commitment to the task is like, you also risk skipping it, as my dad and I ended up doing when we ran this route on a particularly grim 'summer's' day recently. After getting rained on for nearly five hours straight, and barely having been able to see a foot in front of us at any point, Dad declared he was ready for breakfast (a decision I was in full agreement with), and we hotfooted it down to the Grasshopper Cafe in Hope for eggs and toast followed by coffee and cake. Not a decision I regret in any way but if you're determined to do the whole loop including Win Hill in one go, I recommend stacking the odds in your favour, particularly if the weather *isn't* in your favour.

Going in this direction, having first ascended Win Hill and (hopefully) enjoyed stunning views over a landscape rich with heather, you'll make your way on to the Kinder plateau, crossing Grinds Brook and picking your way through the Wool Packs boulders as you traverse its edge. It can get very boggy as you cross the plateau, but you soon make your way on to the Mam Tor ridge (see route 27). This is probably the highlight of the route and another good reason to go in this direction, as it makes for the perfect end to the day.

WALK BRITAIN

1 Cam High Road   2 Near Laddow Rocks
3 Gargrave   All photos © Jon Barton

30 Pennine Way

> CATEGORY **Multi-day**   DISTANCE **431km**   ASCENT **9,500m**   START **Edale**   FINISH **Kirk Yetholm**
> PUBLIC TRANSPORT **Outbound: train to Edale, via Sheffield or Manchester. Return: bus to Kelso then bus to Berwick-upon-Tweed to pick up mainline railway services. (A bit faffy but worth it for the adventure!)**
> MORE INFORMATION www.nationaltrail.co.uk

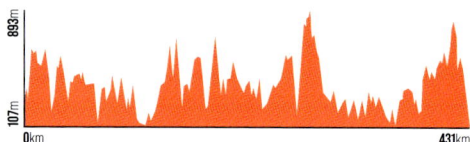

At 431 kilometres long, the Pennine Way gives you the chance to explore the backbone of Britain – and it begins right in the heart of the Hope Valley, in Edale. Some people will choose to tackle it in stages over multiple years, others will complete it as an impressive through-hike, and the very brave will take it on all in one go as part of the Spine Race (the even braver will attempt the infamous Winter Spine, often thought of as one of the UK's hardest ultras).

Whichever approach you choose, in exchange for braving the remoteness and the ever-present risk of wet socks, this pilgrimage through the centre of Britain guarantees you an adventure. For a taster of the full thing, the Peak District section of this trail will give you a slightly more palatable 45 kilometres – ideal for a weekend. You will face some remote stretches without easy access to amenities and your best bet/only real option for splitting this up is to stop in Crowden. You'll then need to veer off the Pennine Way to Marsden at the end in order to pick up a train connection home.

For those carrying on, you'll then continue through Yorkshire and the North Pennines before heading into the Scottish Borders. The North Pennines are a gloriously underrated area of the country, but also sadly extremely lacking in public transport, so completing the Pennine Way is a great way to explore the area without a car. For more information on some of the Yorkshire Dales sections, head to the next section.

If you liked this
The Hope Valley sits more to the north of the Peak District, straddling the boundary between the Dark and the White Peak. The White Peak covers gentle, rolling limestone countryside and can be easily accessed by taking the train to Matlock then using buses (e.g. to Bakewell) to explore the nearby dales. For the Dark Peak, which is typically higher and wilder, travel by train to Glossop and then go from there.

ENGLAND & THE ISLES

Yorkshire Dales

BASE LOCATION **Settle or Horton in Ribblesdale**

WHERE TO STAY **A range of self-catering accommodation and B&Bs in Settle. Campsite and bunkhouse in Horton in Ribblesdale.**

HOW TO GET THERE **Use the Settle–Carlisle Railway for stops in the Ribble Valley. Connections north from Carlisle or south from Leeds.**

When I asked a friend if he fancied coming along to help me research this section, his response immediately confirmed that it was an area worth including. 'Do I get to arrive on the Carlisle to Settle train? That's actually my favourite train line, it's such a good journey.' He's not wrong; it is a fantastic train journey, both for the ride itself and the opportunities it gives you to explore some incredibly scenic spots along the way. The Settle–Carlisle Railway carves its way through the heart of northern England, passing through some of the country's most beloved landscapes and taking in 20 viaducts and 14 tunnels over its 116 kilometres.

But the real beauty lies in where the train stops. With stations dotted throughout the Yorkshire Dales and beyond, you're given ample opportunities to get up close and personal with the beautiful vistas you're travelling through, rather than merely admiring them through a train window. Here I'm focusing on the area around the first few stops on the line: Settle, Horton in Ribblesdale and Ribblehead. With short journey times between stops, it's really up to you where you base yourself. The market town of Settle is larger and has more options for sleeping and eating, but Horton in Ribblesdale is perfect if you're looking for something quieter, with Holme Farm Campsite just a kilometre from the station.

The Yorkshire Dales are known for their rolling hills, expansive moors and quaint villages and these routes will allow you to experience some of the region's best-loved sights. If you want to really immerse yourself in the area, check out the Dales Way, a 127-kilometre trail crossing the Dales and beyond to the Lake District (route 35).

1 On the Dales Way near Starbotton © Stephen Ross **2** Ingleborough from Scales Moor © Stephen Ross
3 Ribblehead Viaduct **4** Bolton Abbey on the Dales Way © Stephen Ross **5** Running through Sulber with Pen-y-ghent behind © Stephen Ross **6** On the Yorkshire Three Peaks © Jon Barton

WALK BRITAIN

1 Attermire Scar © Pete Stuart/Shutterstock.com   2 Ribblehead Viaduct

31 Warrendale Knotts and Attermire Scar

CATEGORY **Short**   DISTANCE **7km**   ASCENT **280m**   START/FINISH **Settle**
PUBLIC TRANSPORT **Both ways: train to/from Settle, if needed**

A key feature of the geography of this area is the limestone you find here and this loop around Attermire Scar and Warrendale Knotts from Settle gives you a chance to explore it in various forms. Apparently, this limestone was formed in tropical seas more than 300 million years ago, and while I can't promise you a tropical climate, I can promise some brilliant views over the surrounding countryside on this route.

Starting from Settle station, you'll head out of the town and make your way through some farm tracks and up across open fields – with the Ribble Valley opening up ahead of you – before you turn right and continue to climb. You'll pass Victoria Cave, where a wide range of Bronze Age artefacts have been found over the years (although I'd probably not suggest searching for treasure today). The path then skirts around the limestone outcrops of both Attermire Scar and the nearby Warrendale Knotts before taking you back to Settle. Try the Folly Coffee House if you've worked up an appetite – it's charity-run and they do a great scone.

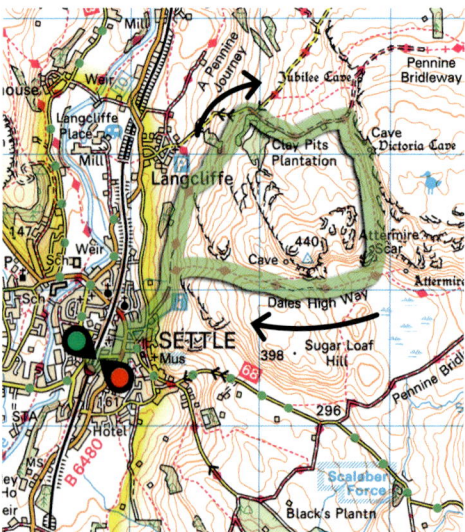

ENGLAND & THE ISLES

32 Whernside and the Ribblehead Viaduct

CATEGORY **Medium**   DISTANCE **13km**   ASCENT **450m**   START/FINISH **Ribblehead**
PUBLIC TRANSPORT **Both ways: train to/from Ribblehead**

Whichever way you look at it, the Ribblehead Viaduct is impressive. The Grade II* listed structure stands at more than 30 metres tall and is just as imposing whether you're catching glimpses of it from afar or walking beneath its arches. Beginning this route from Ribblehead station, you'll start by skirting around what was once dubiously named 'Batty Wife Hole' (I'll reserve comment on that one), and then following the railway line into the valley before starting the Whernside climb.

Whernside is one of the Yorkshire Three Peaks (check out route 34 to attempt the hat-trick) and, I think, my favourite of the trio. At 736 metres it's actually the highest point in the Dales but the long, steady climb means you gain the height relatively gently, maximising your chances of enjoying the scenery rather than just thinking about how tired your legs are. Once the bulk of the climb is done, you get to enjoy a fantastic high-level ridge walk with views over to Ingleborough. The descent is steep, and I'd argue it forms the hardest part of the day (it was certainly the section I was slowest on). If you're lucky you'll find an ice cream van at the bottom.

Your final couple of kilometres are flat along the valley floor, eventually taking you under the somewhat intimidating arches of the viaduct and back to the station. It's a good idea to keep an eye on the train times as there can be a bit of a gap between services, but if you do find yourself with a long wait, The Station Inn is perfectly situated for a post-walk pub lunch. Ribblehead station isn't the worst place to wait either, with a visitor centre and coffee shop. Time it right and you might even get to see a steam train!

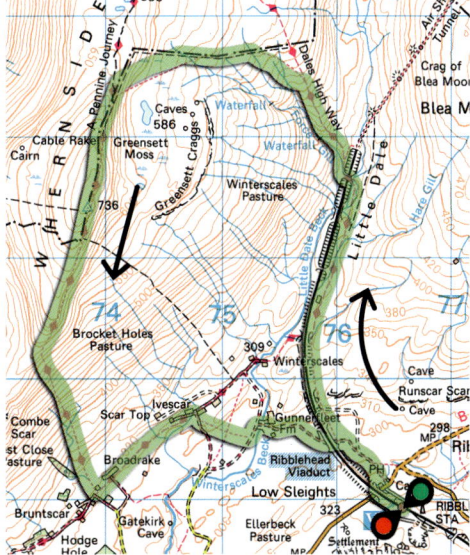

WALK BRITAIN

1 River Ribble next to Stainforth Force © Nicola Pulham/Shutterstock.com
2 Ribblehead station © nikonpete/Shutterstock.com

33 Settle to Ribblehead

CATEGORY **Challenge**   DISTANCE **25km**
ASCENT **450m**   START **Settle**   FINISH **Ribblehead**
PUBLIC TRANSPORT **Outbound: train to Settle if needed. Return: train from Ribblehead.**

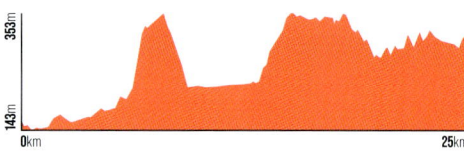

The Ribble Way is 113 kilometres long and follows the River Ribble from its mouth to its source. Many say that this 25-kilometre stretch is the best part of it, as you head right through the heart of the Dales. Beginning in Settle, the natural way to start the day is by heading to Car and Kitchen for a pre-adventure energy boost of coffee and cake. You then need to cross the river to pick up the Ribble Way in Giggleswick (points for a great name – how could you be sad in a place called Giggleswick?), before following the river to Stainforth. On the way you pass Stainforth Force, a cascading waterfall which is a very popular swimming spot in the summer and worth packing your swim gear for.

After Stainforth you have a bit of ascent before picking up the river path again into Horton in Ribblesdale. This is a good place to refuel if you need to, with a couple of pubs and help yourself cups of tea available in the church 'most days' according to the sign I saw (I'm afraid I'm not able to be specific on which days exactly …). From Horton, the Ribble Way climbs again, travelling up to the river's tributaries. This is a really special stretch of trail – you've mostly got a good track underfoot and the views ahead towards Ingleborough and Whernside are stunning. At Gearstones Farm, you leave the Ribble Way and head down the road to Ribblehead station, where the day ends. Road walking generally isn't the most exciting, but the views don't let up here, with the viaduct looming ahead.

You can also easily split this one in two, if you don't fancy such a long day, using Horton in Ribblesdale station as a break point. If you're only going to tackle one half, then I suggest the northern section from Horton to Ribblehead.

1 Ingleborough summit in winter © Stephen Ross 2 Yorkshire Three Peaks signage
3 Nearing the end of the Yorkshire Three Peaks – in Sulber Nick looking towards
Pen-y-ghent © Stephen Ross 4 Limestone flags on the Yorkshire Three Peaks

34 Yorkshire Three Peaks

CATEGORY **Multi-day**   DISTANCE **41km**
ASCENT **1,440m**   START/FINISH **Horton in Ribblesdale**   PUBLIC TRANSPORT **Both ways: train to/from Horton in Ribblesdale, if needed**

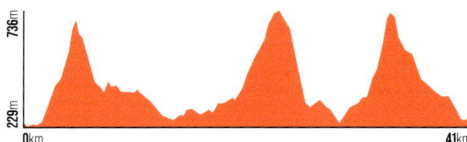

The Yorkshire Three Peaks is a circular route taking in three of the county's tallest hills: Whernside (736 metres), Ingleborough (724 metres) and Pen-y-ghent (694 metres). The first two take the top spots as Yorkshire's highest peaks, with Pen-y-ghent sitting at number nine. Together, the three make up a formidable one-day challenge which enables you to see a fantastic amount of the eastern Yorkshire Dales in one sweep. Most walkers will be happy to finish in under 12 hours, while the current running record, set at the annual Three Peaks fell race, is a staggering 2 hours 46 minutes, set by Andy Peace in 1996. See which end of the spectrum you come out closer to!

This near-marathon-length challenge covers a mixture of well-made paths, limestone pavements and rocky trails, with some sections which will be boggy for most of the year. Starting from the village of Horton in Ribblesdale, you'll immediately launch into the first climb of the day up Pen-y-ghent. Legs firmly awake, some more leisurely miles down to Ribblehead follow – an ideal place to stop for lunch and admire the impressive viaduct and also home to another train station should you want to split the walk up into two days.

From the viaduct you'll head up Whernside, from whose ridge you'll see your whole day span out before you in clear conditions, with Pen-y-ghent to one side and Ingleborough to the other, plus bonus views of the Howgills, Lake District and Morecambe Bay. Back down the other side you'll find a cafe selling not only snacks and drinks but also hats, scarves and gloves for £2 a piece. Ideal if you've lost yours in a gust of wind earlier in the day (not totally outside the realms of possibility if the conditions are anything like when I did the route!).

Stocked up, it's time for the last climb, a real leg burner up one of Ingleborough's steeper sides followed by a short out-and-back to touch the trig point at the top. Then it's just a case of heading back down to Horton in Ribblesdale, working your way through fields of glacially deposited limestone boulders on the way, where a spot in the pub will be waiting for you to toast your achievements.

As a popular charity challenge, the route can get very busy and there were even aid stations set up along the way the weekend I did it. There's something quite nice about the sense of camaraderie I found on the route and it was encouraging to see a diverse mix of people out enjoying the hills (sadly all too often this is not the case). That being said, avoid peak season where possible to help balance out the flow of visitors and skip big queues on the trails. Arriving by public transport is one really helpful way to reduce the pressure on the local area too.

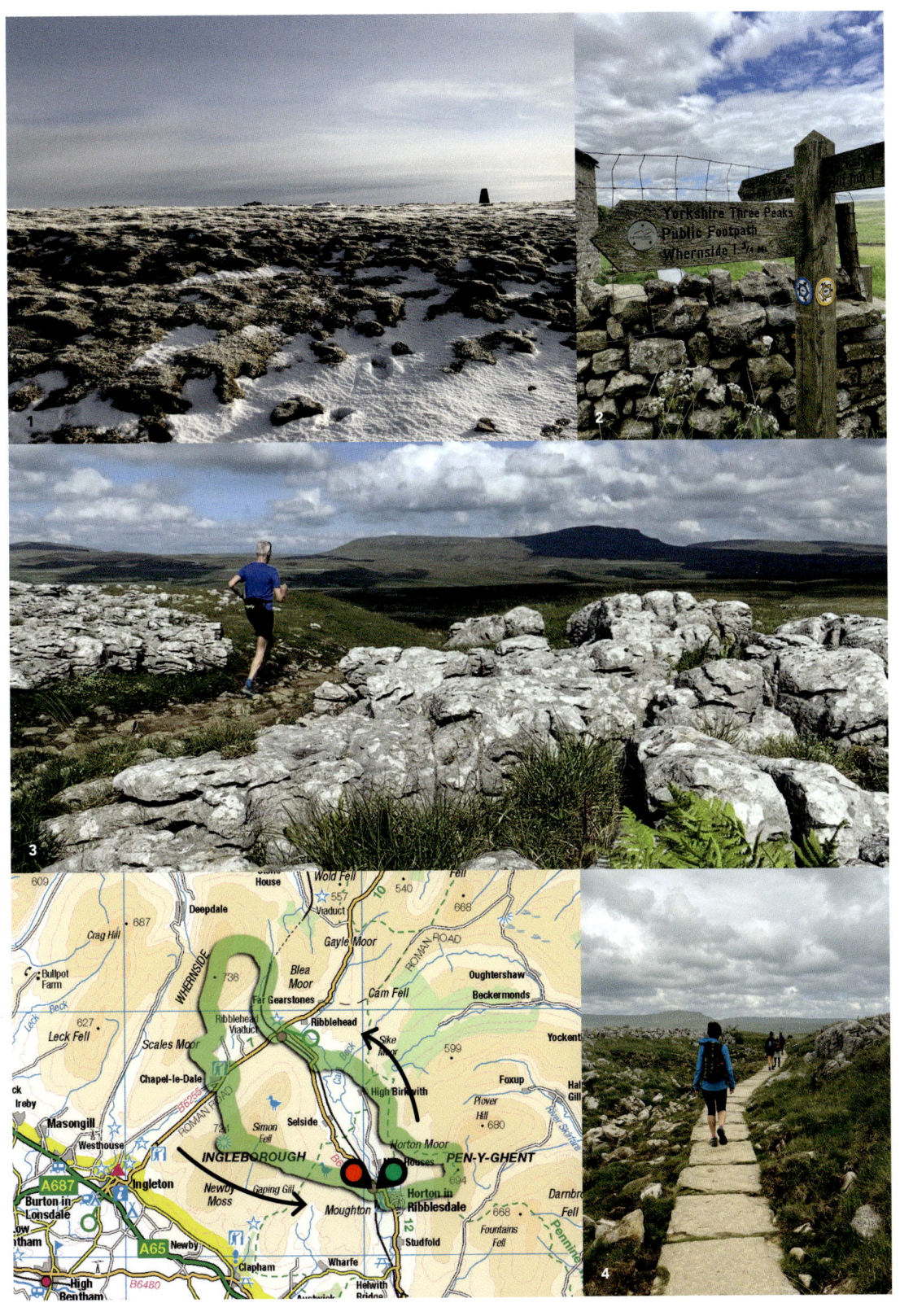

1 On the Dales Way near Sedbergh with the Howgills in the background © Stephen Ross

35 Dales Way

> CATEGORY **Multi-day**   DISTANCE **127km**   ASCENT **1,480m**   START **Ilkley**   FINISH **Bowness-on-Windermere**
> PUBLIC TRANSPORT **Outbound: train to Ilkley. Return: bus to Windermere then onward trains from there.**
> MORE INFORMATION **www.dalesway.org**

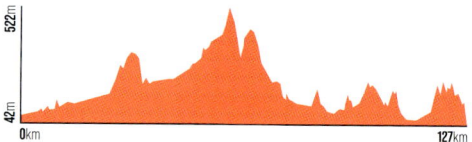

I have several friends who did the Dales Way as their first multi-day hike and in many ways it's the perfect starter trail, as well as still having a lot to offer for the more seasoned walker. At 127 kilometres in length, it's a considerable undertaking (most people complete it in six to ten days), but it covers relatively gentle terrain and is well waymarked throughout. This leaves you to concentrate on the simple act of walking and the all-important task of scouting out the cosiest Dales pub.

Setting off from Ilkley, you'll follow winding riverside trails and footpaths through rolling farmland as you make your way across the Yorkshire Dales and then through the gentle foothills of the southern Lake District. The journey finishes in Bowness-on-Windermere, right on the banks of the great lake. This route isn't just about the natural world though. Along the way you're also treated to sights of the Bolton Abbey ruins and Yockenthwaite Stone Circle, as well as countless drystone walls, Victorian viaducts and enchanting boundary hedgerows.

While the Dales Way is fairly gentle underfoot, one challenge it presents is its remoteness. You'll need to plan accommodation in advance, as options are limited and can get booked up. For more freedom, camping is a good idea.

If you liked this
One way to visit the east of the Yorkshire Dales is to travel by train to Harrogate then catch the bus to Pateley Bridge, a market town which I don't think it's overkill to describe as idyllic. It sits on the edge of the Nidderdale National Landscape; this area of the Dales is well worth visiting, boasting a number of stunning reservoirs (including Gouthwaite, which you can do a lap of from Pateley Bridge) and some of the darkest skies in England, due to the lack of light pollution.

Isle of Man

> BASE LOCATION **Douglas (but the island's buses are so good you can really stay anywhere)**
>
> WHERE TO STAY **Wide range of B&Bs, hotels and self-catering accommodation in Douglas, with campsites all over the island. For bunkhouse accommodation see listings on www.visitisleofman.com**
>
> HOW TO GET THERE **Ferries to Douglas from Liverpool and Heysham, then use local bus and train services to get around the island: www.iombusandrail.im**

The Isle of Man was a last-minute addition to this book. I had only ever heard good things about it but hadn't ever visited until recently (approximately one month before I was due to turn in my already-very-late first draft of this book). After three days on the island, I was not only in wholehearted agreement with all the complimentary things I'd heard but also knew that I *had* to include it. Not only is the island incredibly beautiful and steeped in fascinating history but it also has an impressively well-functioning public transport system. That doesn't just mean plentiful and reliable buses – you can even get a steam train home from one of these routes. Extremely exciting, I hope you'll agree.

There are also plenty of non-bus related reasons I fell so in love with the Isle of Man. Similarly to Arran – and many islands, I suppose – its appeal lies in the variety of landscapes you get in a relatively small package. Think 160 kilometres of coast path circumnavigating the island, prominent peaks (including one official mountain, Snaefell), sandy bays and pebble beaches, ample wildlife spotting opportunities, clear water to swim in, cascading waterfalls, rolling green farmland … Add to that friendly people and delicious local produce and I'm not sure you can really ask for much more.

Perhaps unsurprisingly the coast dominates this section, with most routes incorporating it in one way or another. Although you can fly, I'd strongly urge you to take the ferry instead for a gentler option environmentally. The crossing can be a little rough at times but it's actually much more reliable, with the boats more likely to run in bad weather than the planes. Perhaps the biggest plus is that Douglas Ferry Terminal is directly opposite Noa Bakehouse – a bakery specialising in sourdough bread and sweet treats, who also roast their own coffee, brew their own beer and serve up delicious brunches. You don't get that at the airport!

1 Cronk ny Arrey Laa © Peter Mason **2** Noa Bakehouse pastry **3** Douglas sunset **4** Carved cross on Cronk ny Arrey Laa © Peter Mason **5** Port Erin © Peter Mason **6** Laxey station © Peter Mason

WALK BRITAIN

1 Dhoon Glen © Mustard_Assets/Shutterstock.com

36 Dhoon Glen

CATEGORY **Short** DISTANCE **3km** ASCENT **180m** START/FINISH **Dhoon Glen** PUBLIC TRANSPORT **Both ways: bus or Manx Electric Railway between Douglas and Dhoon Glen (45 minutes)**

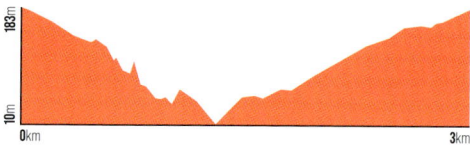

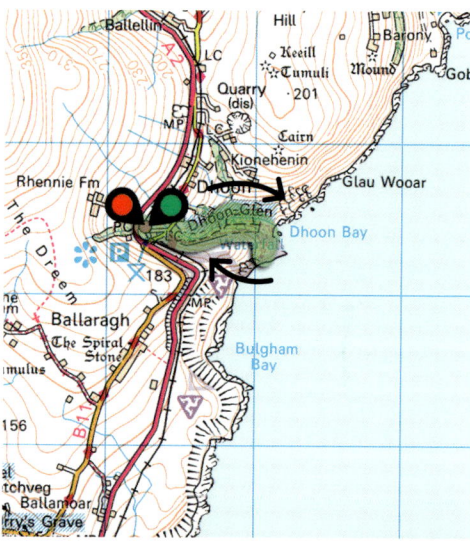

This route is small but mighty, packing a lot into the relatively short distance. Situated towards the north of the island, just south of Ramsey, you can get a bus to Dhoon Glen, but I'd recommend travelling there on the Manx Electric Railway. There's a tuck shop at the station in case you need any extra snacks before you get started on what is 3 kilometres of pure wonder.

Nestled in this narrow glen is one of the Isle of Man's most dramatic waterfalls, which makes it a popular spot for photographers. Once you've taken in the waterfall, you'll continue down the track to Dhoon Bay. The secluded cove is littered with distinctive rock formations and is the ideal place to enjoy a picnic, with the waves crashing around you and seabirds circling overhead. On a good weather day, you can easily extend your outing by whiling away a few hours here before heading over the cliffs and through the enchanted forest back to the station.

Given the length of the walk, you'll probably have some time to spare before or after (if you haven't spent too long at the beach). Make the most of being at this end of the island by hopping back on the railway for a few stops to Ramsey and poke around some of the town's many independent shops.

ENGLAND & THE ISLES

37 Snaefell

CATEGORY **Short**　DISTANCE **8km**　ASCENT **590m**　START **Laxey**　FINISH **Snaefell summit**　PUBLIC TRANSPORT **Outbound: bus or Manx Electric Railway from Douglas to Laxey (30 minutes). Return: Snaefell Mountain Railway from Snaefell summit to Laxey then bus or Manx Electric Railway to Douglas (1 hour 5 minutes).**

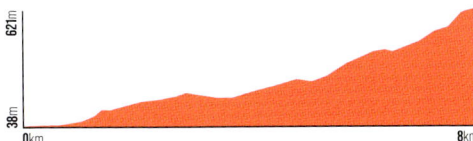

The Isle of Man isn't short of hills but, at 621 metres tall, Snaefell is the only one which achieves mountain status. Not only that but it's also unique in being one of only two mountains in the UK that you can get a train to the top of (the other being Yr Wyddfa – see route 68). However, if you fancy a bit more fresh air with your views, then this route allows you to experience the novelty of the train while also stretching your legs. You have two choices: hike up and then enjoy a ride down as your reward (which I describe here) or take the train up and stroll down. Or, of course, you can skip the train altogether and complete both legs on foot.

Either way, you'll want to start in the town of Laxey on the east coast, home to the largest working waterwheel in the world (which conveniently reopened in 2022). You'll then leave Laxey and the coast behind and head inland past the remnants of derelict mines, which can be a bit eerie, before crossing the famous TT mountain road. From here you make your way across open moorland to the summit where, on a clear day, you'll be able to see all the UK's nations: England, Scotland, Wales and Northern Ireland.

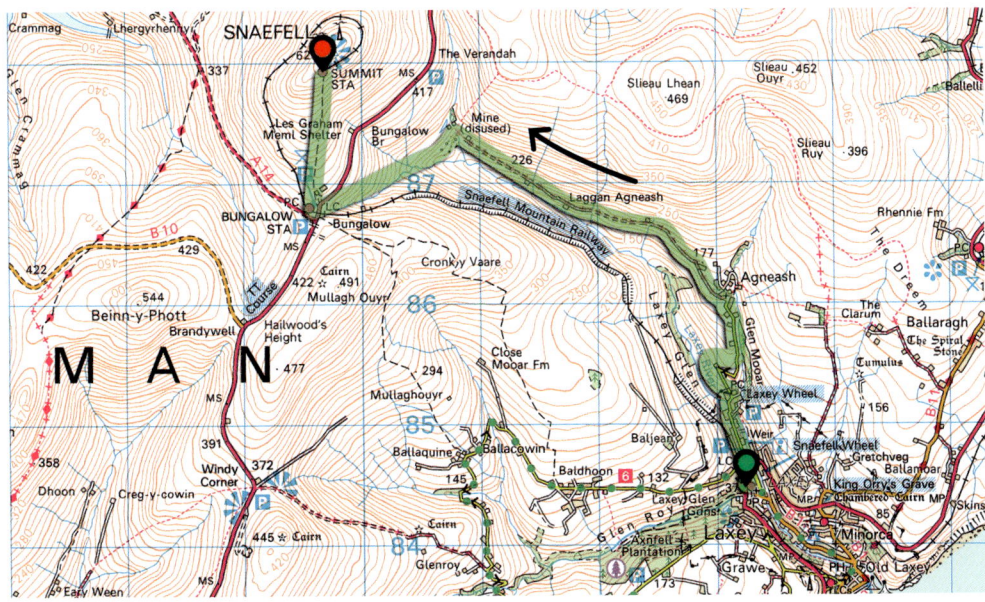

71

1 Calf of Man from the mainland

38 Calf of Man Circular

CATEGORY **Medium**   DISTANCE **14km**
ASCENT **300m**   START/FINISH **Port St Mary**
PUBLIC TRANSPORT **Both ways: bus or Isle of Man Steam Railway between Douglas and Port St Mary (45 minutes/1 hour 5 minutes)**

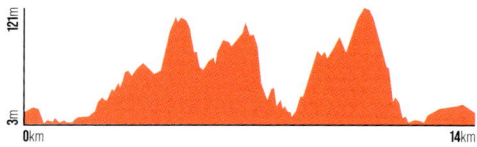

The Calf of Man is a smaller island located 600 metres from the southern tip of the Isle of Man. Perched in this spectacular spot, you can visit the island itself and even stay overnight at the Calf of Man Bird Observatory hostel during the summer months. It's a haven for birdwatchers, with more than 33 species of birds breeding on the island, including the Manx shearwater. These are incredible creatures who somehow manage to return from their annual migration and, under the cover of darkness, find their way back to their own underground burrows. And the stakes are high: their short legs mean that they must fly directly into the correct nest, as they can't just walk a few metres to the right one if they aim wrong. This has remained my number one nature fact ever since somebody first told me about Manx shearwaters a few years ago.

We're not going over to the Calf of Man during this route but instead admiring it from a distance. Incidentally, I was politely corrected by somebody when I referred to 'the mainland', meaning England, Wales and Scotland; to Manx people the Isle of Man is the mainland, and the Calf of Man is the island. Something to be aware of if you're trying to get home!

This circular route begins at Port St Mary station, meaning you can travel there or back – or both – by steam train if you're staying somewhere along the trainline to Douglas. An absolutely delightful way to begin an adventure! Following the coastal path all the way around the peninsula in a clockwise direction, one of the highlights on this route is the Sugarloaf, a 50-metre-high sea stack which itself is home to many breeding seabirds and was first climbed in 1933 by pioneering climber Dr A.W. Kelly. You'll also pass the Chasms, deep crevices in the rock which make for a dramatic sight.

Continuing on, you'll soon reach the *pièce de résistance*: the Calf of Man itself. You're almost guaranteed to see seals here pretty much all year round so bring your binoculars. Stop at the Sound Cafe for a break (I recommend a crab sandwich) before completing your loop and finishing back at Port St Mary.

1 Cronk ny Arrey Laa **2** View over Peel **3** Cronk ny Arrey Laa

39 Peel to Port Erin

CATEGORY **Long** DISTANCE **24km**
ASCENT **1,030m** START **Peel** FINISH **Port Erin**
PUBLIC TRANSPORT **Outbound: bus from Douglas to Peel (35 minutes). Return: bus or Isle of Man Steam Railway from Port Erin to Douglas (1 hour/ 1 hour 5 minutes).**

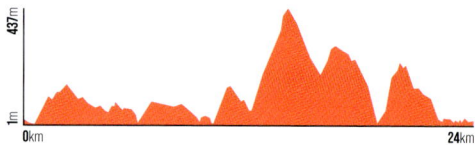

I ran this 24-kilometre stretch of the Raad ny Foillan coast path while visiting for Manx Litfest (a fantastic event normally held in September that I highly recommend coinciding your trip to the Isle of Man with if possible). I had the Sunday free so took the bus to Peel from Douglas and ran down to Port Erin. It was October 1st but felt like summer and at the end of the run I went for a sea swim in my running kit and then ate fish and chips on the beach before catching the steam train back to Douglas. An absolutely glorious way to see in a new month and worth the soggy shorts on the way home.

Coast paths are often pretty hilly and this stretch especially so! Not only do you have the usual up and down (beginning right away as you leave Peel's picturesque harbour behind you and ascend Corrins Hill) but you also climb Cronk ny Arrey Laa, one of the highest points on this part of the island. This 437-metre hill drops directly into the Irish Sea and makes for an imposing sight as you approach it, as well as offering a fantastic vantage point from the summit. I had one of those magical moments at the top where the dense cloud I'd been climbing through (a tiny bit of bad weather in a day that was otherwise wall-to-wall sunshine) shifted, revealing the trail snaking over the cliffs ahead and the sea stretching out to the horizon as I ran down.

This trail can be slow going in places. Not only do you have several more notable climbs to tackle, but the path could do with a little TLC and is overgrown in places. I came home covered in scratches (that's trail running, I suppose) but they were more than worth it for the full day of sunshine and sea air. It's one of those dramatic sections of coast that somehow makes you instantly feel at one with nature, if you'll forgive me for how whimsical that sounds.

A highlight is Fleshwick Bay, a quiet cove that I had all to myself. From here there was one last steep bit, up Bradda Hill, before the final descent into Port Erin. Passing the impressive Milner's Tower the village soon comes into sight, remaining so until the very end. The route ends here but the fun really begins, with all the fish and chips and sea swimming and travelling on steam trains that I mentioned earlier. Pop into Bridge Bookshop in Port Erin if you get the chance – it's one of two branches of the family run bookshop (the other being in Ramsey) that has been selling books for more than 50 years. For an extra special post-walk treat, book a slot in the wood-fired sauna on the beach: **www.kishteycheh.im**

40 Raad ny Foillan

> CATEGORY **Multi-day**   DISTANCE **158km**   ASCENT **2,500m**   START/FINISH **Douglas, or anywhere on the coast. As it's a complete circuit, it doesn't really matter where you start.**

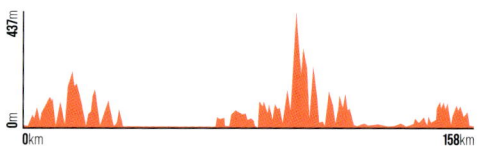

Raad ny Foillan is Manx Gaelic for 'Way of the Gull'; you'll follow signs with gulls on as you circumnavigate the island. At 158 kilometres in length, this long-distance trail gives you the chance to walk a lap of an entire nation, in a stint you could reasonably take as annual leave. The official *Raad ny Foillan Coastal Footpath* guide (available at www.visitisleofman.com) splits the route into a fairly leisurely 12 stages but runners or fastpackers may want to challenge themselves to complete it over a long weekend.

Perhaps the best thing about this route is the variety it offers. The Isle of Man is sometimes described as 'Britain in Miniature', but I think this does it a disservice. The Isle of Man isn't simply a smaller-scale recreation of something larger but, rather, a place which is special in its own right. In a single day you can experience everything from spectacular clifftop trails to long sandy beaches, secluded wildlife havens to busy promenades selling ice cream, or open farmland to narrow wooded glens.

The fantastic Bus Vannin network means you could quite easily choose to stay in one place on the coast (Douglas would make the most sense) and travel between stages using the bus. Alternatively, you can approach the trail as a through-hike and camp along the way. Whichever style of adventure you choose, there's something incredibly satisfying about completing a lap of an island, and I've no doubt you'll board the ferry home basking in the glory of a job well done.

> ### If you liked this
> Islands naturally lend themselves to car-free adventures. Everybody has to get the ferry there anyway and it's normally much cheaper to travel as a foot passenger. As well as the Isle of Arran (see pages 144–153), another one to look at is the Isle of Wight. I spent a miraculously sunny three days walking its coast path a few years ago and it made for a brilliant bank holiday adventure. Gorgeous clifftop trails, swim spots aplenty and some truly delicious cheese scones at a hotel in Ventnor for a special mid-walk treat. Delightful. You can get the ferry over from either Portsmouth or Lymington, making it convenient for anybody based in the south. I was living in London at the time and managed to stay on the Isle of Wight on Sunday night, catch an early ferry back and be at my desk for nine o'clock on Monday morning.

Lake District

> BASE LOCATION **Ambleside**
>
> WHERE TO STAY **Wide range of B&Bs and self-catering accommodation in Ambleside. YHA Ambleside is right on the banks of Windermere. The easiest campsite to get to from Ambleside is at Rydal Hall (a short bus ride from the town).**
>
> HOW TO GET THERE **Train to Windermere (you'll probably need to change at Oxenholme Lake District) then use local bus services. The 555 bus between Windermere and Keswick will be your best friend!**

When I told my auntie that I was planning to move up to the Lake District, her first response was, 'Oh yes, I like the buses there'. Admittedly they're not normally seen as the key attraction of the area, which is better known for its mountains and, of course, lakes, but I have to agree with her that they're pretty good. In fact, in many ways it was the public transport connections to and through the Lake District that inspired this book.

Perhaps I'm biased, given that I live here, but I just don't think there are many places in the world better for an adventure than the Lake District. Our mountains might not be the tallest you'll find but you can see that as an advantage. The lowest Wainwright is just 290 metres high (Castle Crag, not included this book but accessible by bus from Keswick) and affords you the opportunity to stand atop something significant without clocking up thousands of metres of climbing or needing technical mountaineering skills, as you do to summit in other parts of the world.

With 214 Wainwrights and numerous other fells, 16 larger lakes, around 200 tarns and thousands of kilometres of trails to explore you're unlikely to get bored, but it's not just what's on offer outdoors that makes the Lake District special. Make sure to save some time for the pubs with open fires, the locally brewed beers, the cosy cafes to hide from the rain in and the area's deep literary history (everyone from William Wordsworth to Beatrix Potter called Cumbria home). Even Taylor Swift has a song about Windermere.

I've tried to include a bit of everything in this chapter, from classic mountain routes to lakeside loops, but please know this is a mere taster of what's on offer and I urge you to come back and explore more. I've chosen Ambleside as the base location due to its combination of good public transport links, the array of accommodation options and the amount of walks you can do from the doorstep.

1 Orrest Head **2** Fairfield Horseshoe in the snow **3** Lake District trails
4 View over the Kentmere Horseshoe **5** Cumbria Way **6** Herdwick sheep

41 Orrest Head

CATEGORY **Short** DISTANCE **4km** ASCENT **130m** START/FINISH **Windermere**
PUBLIC TRANSPORT **Both ways: buses between Ambleside and Windermere (15 minutes)**

Orrest Head is the small (in Lake District terms) hill perched behind Windermere town; the trail begins almost directly from the train station. This walk was actually Alfred Wainwright's first introduction to the Lake District. The view went on to inspire the legacy he ultimately left; his volumes of writing about the fells (typically now simply known as Wainwrights) are generally considered the standard reference for the area.

Not only does the Orrest Head walk come endorsed by Wainwright but it's also one of the Lake District National Park's official Miles without Stiles routes. There are a few different trails which peel off from the main track, but make sure you follow the blue signs for the accessible route which is suitable for wheelchairs, pushchairs and scooters. There are still steep sections but the effort of getting up is more than worth it once you emerge from the woodland and see the panoramic views over Windermere.

Wainwright described the unveiling of this landscape as being 'As though a curtain had dramatically been torn aside, beheld a truly magnificent view'; I won't try and say it better myself. To really put yourself in his footsteps, I recommend listening to Wainwright's episode of *Desert Island Discs* as you walk.

ENGLAND & THE ISLES

42 Grasmere and Rydal Water

CATEGORY **Medium**   DISTANCE **9km**   ASCENT **160m**   START/FINISH **Grasmere**
PUBLIC TRANSPORT **Both ways: buses between Ambleside and Grasmere (15 minutes)**

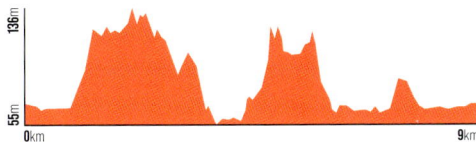

This circular walk around Grasmere and Rydal Water was the first walk I ever did in the Lake District, on a trip with my dad well over ten years ago. He always says that it's the walk he'd take somebody who didn't like walking on, to try and convince them as to its merits. Given that I had little more than a passing interest in the outdoors the first time I did it and now I live in the Lakes, I suppose I have to conclude that his theory proved to be true. It's definitely still the route I've done most often, whether walking with others or as a solo run. As a low-level route, it's ideal for days when the weather isn't so good.

Starting in Grasmere village and travelling clockwise you first follow the Coffin Route. Historically this trail was used to carry the dead from Rydal to the church in Grasmere, but these days it makes for a nice walk despite the morbid undertones. Where the trees clear on your right-hand side, views of the lake appear and you can see the peaks on the other side of it. Dropping down to Rydal, you can stop at Rydal Hall for coffee, cakes and toilets before crossing the road and hugging the shores of both lakes on your return to Grasmere village. You'll pass several swim spots so pack your kit for a refreshing dip.

If you're feeling energetic, you can add on an ascent of Loughrigg Fell. I've got a really soft spot for Loughrigg despite (or perhaps because of) its modest height of 335 metres.

Loughrigg is fantastic for autumn hikes where the criss-crossing trails around the summit paint a kaleidoscope of colours, a winter's afternoon run where you can time your descent perfectly with golden hour to see the valleys below bathed in crisp sunshine, or summer heatwave expeditions featuring a dip in Loughrigg Tarn – it's proof that bigger isn't always better.

Regardless of whether you choose to do the extra climb or not, this route ranks highly on the effort-to-reward scale. And whatever you do, make sure you don't miss the famous Grasmere Gingerbread® at the end. Sold for nearly 200 years, you'll find a queue outside the shop at pretty much any time of day. Even if you normally prefer to avoid the crowds, this is one queue worth joining.

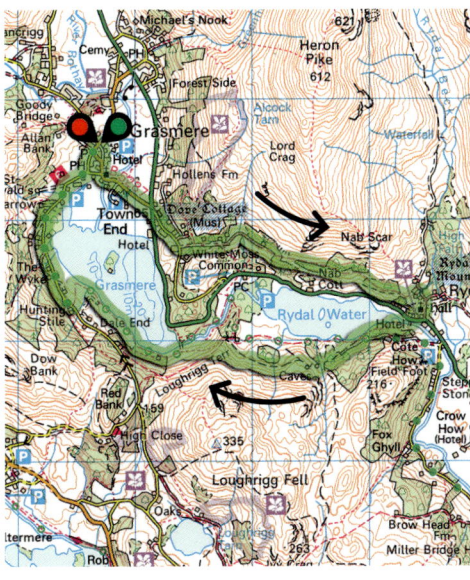

43 Fairfield Horseshoe

CATEGORY **Long**   DISTANCE **18km**
ASCENT **890m**   START/FINISH **Ambleside**

The Fairfield Horseshoe is a classic Lakeland route, and for good reason. Starting from Ambleside, the loop will take you over eight Wainwrights: Fairfield, of course, the main peak for the day, but also Low Pike, High Pike, Dove Crag, Hart Crag, Great Rigg, Heron Pike and Nab Scar.

While the current record of just under 75 minutes for the Fairfield Horseshoe Fell Race might have you believe otherwise, the underfoot terrain of this route can be challenging. Easing you in with a somewhat false sense of security on a gentle lane out of Ambleside, you'll soon find yourself navigating rocky paths and boggy sections, including some light scrambling on Hart Crag. But the 360-degree panorama you'll be treated to on a clear day makes it worth it.

Once you've completed the route, to see your achievement from another angle take the bus to Rydal and walk the kilometre or so up past Rydal Falls to Buckstones Jump. Nestled in the Fairfield Valley, you can swim in the plunge pool and get a completely different perspective on the horseshoe route.

1–3 High Street

44 Windermere to Penrith over High Street

CATEGORY **Challenge**   DISTANCE **39km**
ASCENT **1,110m**   START **Windermere**
FINISH **Penrith**   PUBLIC TRANSPORT **Train and bus connections to Windermere and from Penrith**

I just think there's something that always feels undeniably epic about a point-to-point route. You pack your bag with snacks and layers (vital in the Lake District where you can easily experience four seasons in one day) and then you set off on an adventure, each footstep taking you towards your goal. And it can surely only add to the excitement knowing that you're following in the footsteps of the Romans, as you are on this route.

This 2,000-year-old road is believed to have been built by the Romans to link forts in Penrith and Ambleside; today you can still see remnants of old kerb stones as you traverse the high fells. It's a little ambiguous as to where exactly the Roman road begins and ends, but for ease of public transport, our route starts at Windermere station and finishes at Penrith station. This gives you a 39-kilometre day out, featuring some stunning sections of Lakeland trail.

The weeks leading up to doing this route were some of the wettest I've ever experienced in the Lakes. I thought Kirsty and I were guaranteed a soaking as the date in our diaries approached with no sign of the weather letting up. Kirsty is also the commissioning editor of this book, and I think we can all agree that going on six-hour-long runs in the pouring rain with authors perhaps goes above and beyond the call of duty! Luckily, we were afforded one dry day amidst the deluge which allowed us to enjoy the scenery, so I won't feel *too* guilty for roping Kirsty into my book research.

Setting off from Windermere you first climb up to Orrest Head (see route 41) then you make your way across farmland before climbing up to the fell section. You trace the same route as the western half of the Kentmere Horseshoe, which is actually one of my favourite stretches of trail in the Lakes. It's worth looking over your shoulder as you pick your way across this section, because the views back along the ridge over Yoke, Ill Bell and Froswick are pretty special. Continuing on you reach High Street, this route's namesake and high point.

With High Street ticked off, you've done the bulk of the climbing, and from here you've got a mostly downhill journey to finish. Keep looking left and right as different lakes come into view, from Blea Water and Hayeswater up high to the mighty Ullswater as you start to descend. Speaking of water, this route can be boggy so consider that when you're choosing your footwear.

It's perhaps stating the obvious to tell you that this is a long route. For slightly less of a challenge, your first option is to split it over two days with a wild camp. The other is to chop off either end – I've done a 28-kilometre version between Troutbeck and Pooley Bridge (bus connections to either end), which without doubt covers the best of the route. If you're in it for the long haul, then continue on past Sockbridge, cross the River Eamont and walk into Penrith. You officially finish at the castle, which is opposite the station, but it's worth heading into town for some much-deserved food. Try Chapter 12 Coffee Rooms for their impressively large scones.

1 Great Lingy Hut, High Pike   2–3 Cumbria Way trails

45 Cumbria Way

CATEGORY **Multi-day**   DISTANCE **112km**   ASCENT **2,800m**   START **Ulverston**   FINISH **Carlisle**
PUBLIC TRANSPORT **Outbound: trains to Ulverston. Return: trains from Carlisle.**   MORE INFORMATION **www.cumbriaway.co.uk**

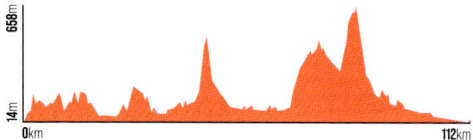

Setting off from Ulverston and taking you all the way north to Carlisle, the Cumbria Way is a 112-kilometre route through the entire Lake District National Park. Compared to other routes in this area, it's a relatively low-level walk (or trail run, if you prefer) meaning you get to see a huge amount of the Lake District while avoiding too much climbing. This also means you're less dictated to by the weather than you might be on more mountainous routes.

The week I walked the Cumbria Way I was lucky to have near-perfect conditions – and admittedly perhaps this skews my view of the experience, but I remember it as one of my all-time-favourite weeks outside. Even the one day of torrential rain is shrouded in positive memories after stumbling across a tea room serving scones halfway through the day, swimming in Derwent Water as the clouds cleared in the late afternoon and then devouring a YHA sticky toffee pudding at the end. Anyway, it's hardly a real Lakeland adventure without at least one proper soaking, is it?

Day after day of postcard-worthy mountain backdrops, numerous lakes, tarns and becks to cool off in, a variety of terrain from low-level farmland and woodland trails to high passes and villages, cafes and pubs scattered along the way for refuelling … the Cumbria Way has everything you need for a genuinely enjoyable week outside. With only two big climbs and plenty of amenities, the Cumbria Way would make a fantastic introduction for somebody new to multi-day hiking.

The route is traditionally split into five stages, with four of those clocking in at around 24 kilometres and then one shorter day. However, you really can choose your own adventure with this one. For a bigger challenge you could fastpack the route over two or three days or even have a crack at running it in one go, while others will choose a more relaxed eight-day schedule. I camped most nights but there are plenty of accommodation options along the way, and you can even opt for baggage transfers to lighten the load. You can find more information and outline schedules on the official Cumbria Way website.

If you liked this
As I've mentioned, the Lake District is surprisingly well served by buses meaning you'll easily be able to discover more parts of the national park on your next trip. Another good base location would be Keswick, which is only a 40-minute bus ride from Penrith station. Keswick is right on the edge of Derwent Water, and you'll have some great walks on your doorstep (try Cat Bells, Skiddaw, Latrigg or Walla Crag). Another option is to take the bus from Penrith to Pooley Bridge instead, and explore the area around Ullswater.

North York Moors

BASE LOCATION **Anywhere on the Esk Valley Railway will give you easy access to all the routes in this section**

WHERE TO STAY **Great Ayton is a large village and has a good range of accommodation. There are good pubs with rooms in Castleton, Danby and Lealholm. Lawnsgate Campsite – a great back-to-basics site – is 2km from Lealholm station. YHA in Whitby.**

HOW TO GET THERE **Train to Middlesbrough then train to villages along the Esk Valley Railway**

When it comes to the variety offered within a single national park, it's hard to beat the North York Moors. Within its 1,436 square kilometres you'll find everything from dramatic coastline and sweeping moorland plateaus to ancient woodlands tucked into quiet dales dotted with sleepy villages. If you're feeling indecisive when you plan your trip, then this is the ideal place to head to. One day you can be breathing in sea air on a clifftop trail, the next losing yourself in acres of heather moorland (which covers an area of around one third of the national park).

The Esk Valley Railway makes it easy to get around. It takes you from Middlesbrough (making for a straightforward connection to mainline services) all the way across the moors to the Yorkshire Coast. Most of the routes in this section focus on exploring the inland moors but if you fancy a coastal hike, simply take the train to Whitby and walk 12 kilometres south to Robin Hood's Bay for a guaranteed good time. A 25-minute bus ride will land you back in Whitby, where I *highly* recommend stopping off at the Magpie Cafe for some of the best fish and chips you'll ever eat.

The magic of the North York Moors won't be lost on you at any time of the year, but I think it really comes into its own during cosy season. As the temperatures drop through autumn and winter, this is the place to be, with ample opportunities to retreat to a fireside table in a village pub after a day outside, cheeks red from the elements and toes grateful for a warm pair of socks. Being outside is great and all, but sometimes nothing quite beats coming inside again.

1 Cleveland Way © Jon Barton   **2** Robin Hood's Bay © Jon Barton   **3–4** Esk Valley © Jon Barton
5 Roseberry Topping © Dave Parry   **6** Near Goathland © Jon Barton

WALK BRITAIN

1 Steam train on the North Yorkshire Moors Railway © Jon Barton   2 View from Roseberry Topping © Dave Parry

46 Grosmont to Goathland

CATEGORY **Short**   DISTANCE **6km**   ASCENT **120m**   START **Grosmont**   FINISH **Goathland**   PUBLIC TRANSPORT Outbound: train to Grosmont on the Esk Valley Railway. Return: steam train on the North Yorkshire Moors Railway from Goathland back to Grosmont, then onwards.   MORE INFORMATION www.nymr.co.uk

This route is all about trains. You'll set off from Grosmont station on the Esk Valley Railway, walk alongside the North Yorkshire Moors Railway line (opened in 1836, this is one of the country's very earliest railways; it is now a popular heritage line) to Goathland station, and then you catch the steam train back to your starting point. Most of this 6-kilometre linear route is a designated Miles without Stiles walk, making it a great one to do with the whole family.

It's a simple walk set to an excellent backdrop as you follow the fast-flowing beck, make your way through woodland that's stood for thousands of years and catch glimpses of the rolling pasture you're surrounded by. There's even the option of a pub stop, with the riverside Birch Hall Inn en route. I think it's best to do it this way around, with the walk first and then the treat of a steam train at the end. However, it does mean you're walking gently uphill. For an easier time, catch the train to Goathland then walk back to Grosmont.

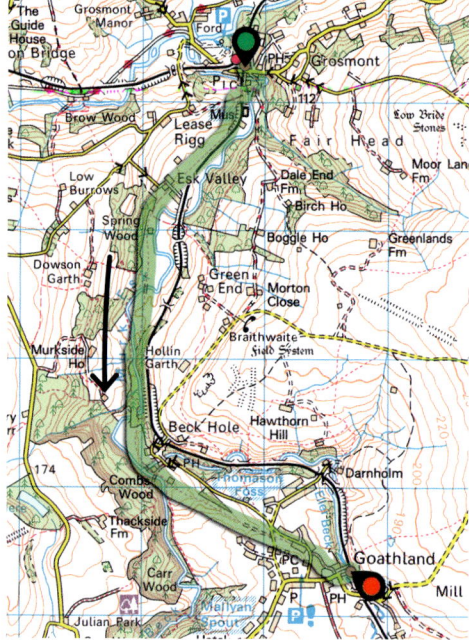

ENGLAND & THE ISLES

47 Roseberry Topping

CATEGORY **Medium**   DISTANCE **10km**   ASCENT **330m**   START/FINISH **Great Ayton**
PUBLIC TRANSPORT **Both ways: train to/from Great Ayton, if needed**

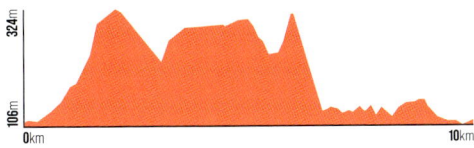

Roseberry Topping is both one of the most recognisable hills on the North York Moors and also one of the most climbed. Erupting rather dramatically from the ground, the hill's distinctive half cone shape has caused it to be nicknamed the 'Yorkshire Matterhorn' (albeit with the Swiss version standing at 14 times the height). It's popular with painters and photographers too, so make sure to take your sketchbook if you're feeling arty (or just your iPhone).

This route begins at Great Ayton station and essentially takes you on a tour around Roseberry Topping, viewing it from a multitude of angles as well as climbing to the summit. At 320 metres tall, it only ranks as the eighth tallest hill on the North York Moors but, towering over the surrounding landscape, it offers you some incredible panoramic views. Visiting in the late summer will give you a chance to see a landscape blanketed with the famous purple heather. Descending from the hill you'll head through Newton Wood, which is a particular treat during bluebell season in April and May. Sadly, this doesn't align with heather season in late summer, so you'll have to use your imagination for one of them.

The walk finishes back at the station but take a wander into Great Ayton village for a look around. Recently named as one of the Best Places to Live by the *Sunday Times*, you'll find its streets full of independent shops and cafes, including the famous Suggitt's ice cream shop.

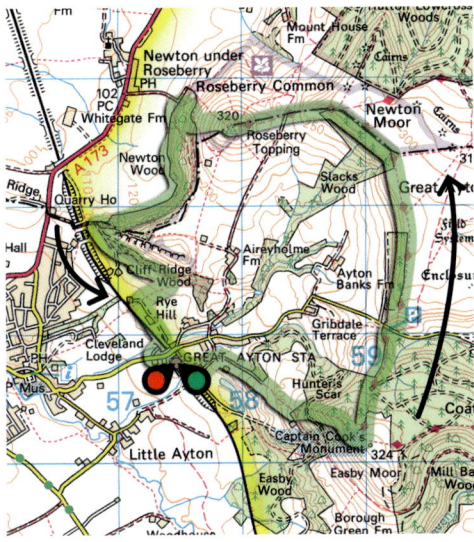

48 Fryup Dales and Danby Beacon

CATEGORY **Long** DISTANCE **20km** ASCENT **570m**
START/FINISH **Danby** PUBLIC TRANSPORT **Both ways: train to/from Danby**

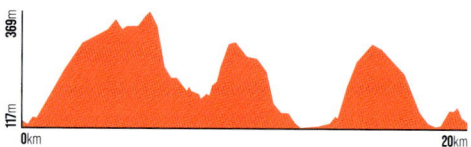

Should you choose a route based on name alone? Perhaps not. But, as a breakfast lover, when I learned about the existence of the Fryup Dales there was no way I wasn't going to include them. Luckily, as well as having fantastic names, they're also very beautiful. This peaceful walk takes you over the ridge dividing Little Fryup Dale and Great Fryup Dale, giving you some spectacular views over both.

As well as enjoying the gentle rolling countryside typical of the area, this route also takes you over Danby Rigg. You've got a good chance of having it to yourself if you visit today but once upon a time this was a busy meeting spot. Keep an eye out for all the prehistoric remains which you can still see, such as Old Wife's Stones, although only one of the original pair still stands. Another highlight of the walk is Danby Beacon, which has stood in some form since Roman times when it served as an important communication and warning tool. Today its elevation makes for a good viewpoint if nothing else.

The route starts and finishes in Danby. About a kilometre before you reach the village, you'll pass Danby Lodge National Park Centre. If all the talk of fry-ups has made you hungry, I'm happy to confirm that the cafe does serve a full English (and a plant-based alternative). Although sadly I do have to tell you that the dales unfortunately aren't actually named after the breakfast dish but instead from Old Norse, with *Friga* being the original settler and *up* from a corruption of 'small valley'. Still, it's a good excuse to eat some hash browns, I reckon.

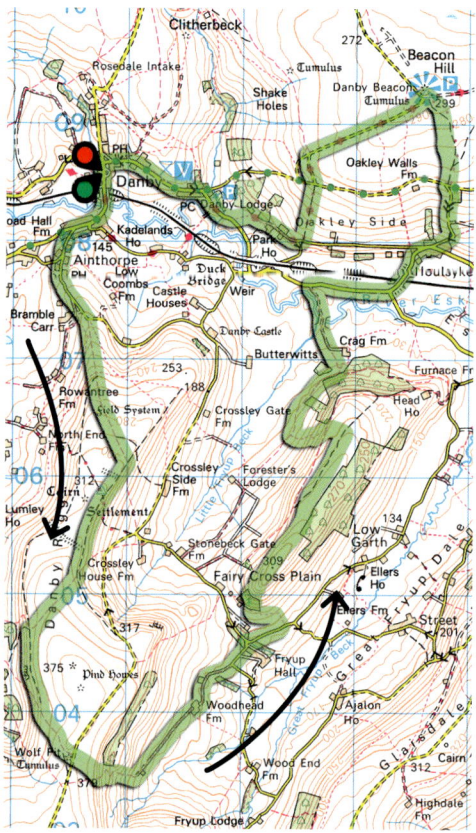

ENGLAND & THE ISLES

49 Esk Valley

CATEGORY **Challenge**   DISTANCE **33km**   ASCENT **450m**   START **Castleton**   FINISH **Whitby**
PUBLIC TRANSPORT **Outbound: trains to Castleton. Return: trains from Whitby.**

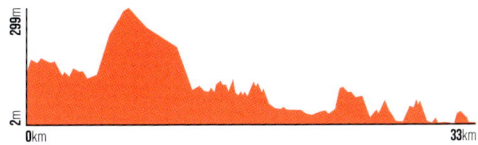

The Esk Valley Walk is a long-distance trail which takes you along the River Esk from source to sea. Starting in Castleton in the heart of the North York Moors, the full route is 59 kilometres long and first involves a loop up to the river source and back to the village, before heading to the coast. We'll be focusing on the latter portion of the route, starting in Castleton and ending in Whitby, which at 33 kilometres long makes for a great standalone long run route or a big day of walking.

You'll be following waymarkers showing a leaping salmon, signifying the fish that live in the river. From start to finish, this route is an absolute feast for the eyes. Beginning surrounded by vibrant moorland and a patchwork of farmers' fields and finishing with the glimmering sea growing ever closer as you approach Whitby, it's a landscape that is guaranteed to make you feel small (in the most grounding sort of way). The latter stages of the route follow the river more closely and you'll also be accompanied by the steam trains chugging along the heritage railway. At the end of the day, you can enjoy some well-deserved fish and chips in Whitby.

If you like the sound of this route and want to have a go at the whole Esk Valley Walk, the fact that it runs close to the railway line of the same name makes it easy to divide into chunks. There are also some fantastic pubs you can stop at along the way. Honourable mention to the Lion Inn at Blakey Ridge, which stands at an elevation of 400 metres and offers incredible views.

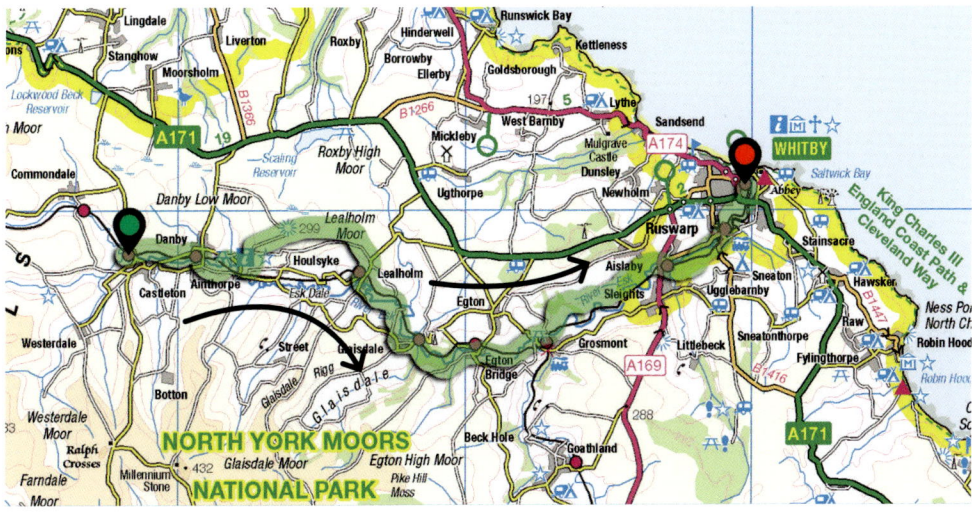

1–3 Cleveland Way © Jon Barton

50 Cleveland Way

CATEGORY **Multi-day**   DISTANCE **175km**   ASCENT **3,310m**   START **Helmsley**   FINISH **Filey**
PUBLIC TRANSPORT **Outbound: train to York then bus to Helmsley. Return: train from Filey.**

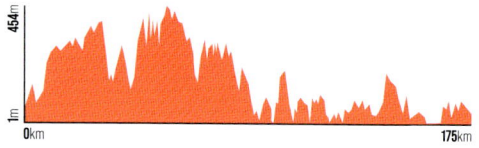

The Cleveland Way hugs the North York Moors for 175 kilometres and gives you the chance to experience the ever-changing landscapes that exist within this national park. It was the second recognised National Trail in England and Wales when it was officially opened in 1969, meaning you'll be following in the footsteps of many other travellers when you embark on your adventure.

Starting in the historic town of Helmsley, you'll hike across the moors before joining up with the rugged coast, passing through Whitby and Scarborough on your way to Filey, where the trail ends. History lovers will enjoy this one too, with important sites such as Helmsley Castle, Rievaulx Abbey, Whitby Abbey and Scarborough Castle dotted along your route. Being relatively low level, this is a good walk all year round but it's perhaps at its best in the early autumn, when you still have a reasonable amount of daylight and the heather is blooming.

If you liked this
The Howardian Hills are a specific National Landscape that sit within the North York Moors, at the southern end of the national park. Fewer than 10,000 people live within the largely unspoiled 204 square kilometres that make up the area. You can take the train to Malton and walk straight into the Howardian Hills from there or travel to York by rail then make use of connecting bus services. There's some good public transport information at www.howardianhills.org.uk

Northumberland

> **BASE LOCATION** Alnwick
>
> **WHERE TO STAY** Wide range of accommodation in Alnwick including YHA Alnwick. Campsites are a bus ride away, including Coast and Castles Camping.
>
> **HOW TO GET THERE** Train to Alnmouth or Morpeth then bus to Alnwick

Sitting on the north-east shoulder of England, just south of the Scottish border, Northumberland is the place to come if you're looking for peace and quiet. It has been officially deemed the quietest county in England, thanks to its low population density.

When I picture Northumberland, the image that immediately comes to mind for me is that of vast sandy beaches and crystal-clear water, and it's this coastal area – the Northumberland Coast National Landscape – which is the focus for this chapter. Boasting some of the cleanest seawater in the country, 100 kilometres of stunning coastal path and supposedly the best kippers you'll find anywhere, I think that Northumberland should be high on your list of places to visit if you're looking for a dose of sea air. It's also a little flatter than some of the other coastal adventures included in this book (I'm looking at you, Dorset), meaning you get all the reward for slightly less exertion.

But if you're in the market for some hills, then don't worry. Venture inland a little and you'll find Northumberland National Park, which covers 1,050 square kilometres of moorland. It is reportedly England's most remote national park, as well as being a designated Dark Sky Park. The remoteness of Northumberland in general doesn't always lend itself to car-free travel but for ease of getting around, I suggest staying in the historic town of Alnwick, which is a short bus ride from train services in Alnmouth plus has bus services to help you explore around the coast and inland.

---

1 Kippers at Low Newton-by-the-Sea © Helen Parry **2** Embleton Bay **3** Dunstanburgh Castle
4 Beadnell lime kilns © Helen Parry **5** Old pillbox in the dunes near Bamburgh © Dave Parry **6** Crab sandwich at Craster

WALK BRITAIN

1 Alnmouth © Robert Harding Video/Shutterstock.com

51 Alnmouth and the River Aln

CATEGORY **Short** DISTANCE **8km** ASCENT **40m** START/FINISH **Lesbury**
PUBLIC TRANSPORT **Both ways: buses between Alnwick and Lesbury (10 minutes)**

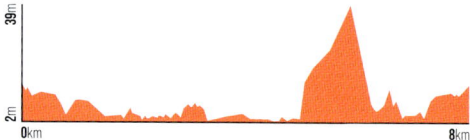

Named after its position at the mouth of the River Aln, Alnmouth is one of many picturesque villages dotted along the Northumberland Coast. Its position tucked into the corner between the Aln Estuary and the wider coastline means that a rich variety of wildlife calls Alnmouth home, some of which you'll hopefully be lucky enough to see on this route.

Walking through the pretty village of Lesbury then across fields leads to a short road section and on to the River Aln. The area around the estuary is part of the Alnmouth Saltmarsh and Dunes Site of Special Scientific Interest – its saltmarshes and reedbeds provide a sanctuary for many migrating and wintering birds. Pick up the River Aln path towards Alnmouth and the coast, where the sand dunes make for another excellent birdwatching spot.

Make some time to have a look around Alnmouth too – the village is famed for its distinctive coloured houses and the High Street is dotted with coffee shops, pubs and shops ready to welcome you. Then it's time for a gentle stroll along the beach and back over fields to Lesbury.

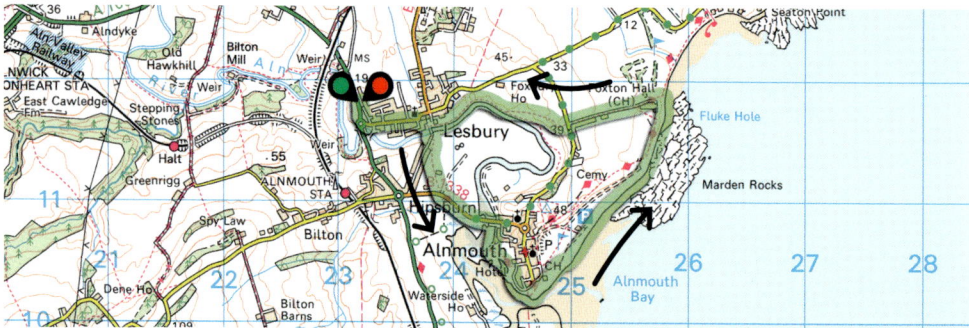

52 Dunstanburgh Castle

CATEGORY **Medium**   DISTANCE **12km**   ASCENT **50m**   START/FINISH **Craster**
PUBLIC TRANSPORT **Both ways: buses between Alnwick and Craster (35 minutes)**

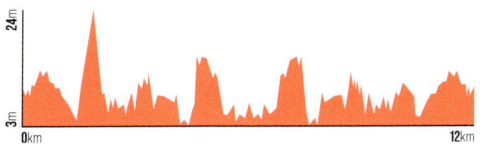

There are more than 70 castles across Northumberland, from those which are still fully functioning like Alnwick (the second largest inhabited castle in the UK, but perhaps best known for *Harry Potter* and *Downton Abbey* being filmed there) to medieval ruins like Dunstanburgh. This out-and-back route allows you to see the latter from every angle. Do your best job of imagining the grand building that once stood there, built during King Edward II's reign in the 14th century. It's nice enough just wandering around the outside but you can also pay to go inside (buy tickets from www.english-heritage.org.uk).

It's not just the castle ruins that this route has going for it though. Alongside the general beauty of this stretch of coast (which is there in abundance, especially on a sunny day), you also have the chance to see basking seals if you're lucky, and a high chance of spotting seabirds depending on the time of year. Swimmers should definitely stop off for a dip in Embleton Bay, which was the highlight of my walk. The sand is soft, and the water is crystal clear. Being an out-and-back route you do, of course, have the flexibility to turn around whenever you like but I recommend carrying on as far as Low Newton-by-the-Sea and stopping off for a break at The Ship Inn. This pub dates back to the 18th century and today has its own microbrewery on site.

Back in Craster, anybody with even a vague liking of fish will want to head to L. Robson and Sons for a Craster kipper. They also do crab sandwiches and other snacks to take away, which in my opinion taste best eaten on the harbour wall. It was rammed here last time I visited due to a crime drama being filmed at the time, but I imagine you'll get a little more peace and quiet when you visit.

53 Simonside Hills

CATEGORY **Long**   DISTANCE **18km**   ASCENT **440m**   START/FINISH **Rothbury**   PUBLIC TRANSPORT **Both ways: buses between Alnwick and Rothbury (change at Morpeth; 1 hour 30 minutes)**

Although I've focused on the coast more in this section, I couldn't help but include a route that allows you to get a taste of the inland part of Northumberland too. It sadly isn't the easiest place to explore by public transport but heading to Rothbury is one fairly straightforward way to do it. This bustling market town acts as a gateway to the moors and is accessible via bus from Alnwick.

On this circular route around the Simonside Hills, you'll see the type of landscape this area is famous for: heather-coated moors, rocky tors and rugged trails. From the high points you'll be able to see even more of the county, with 360-degree views giving you glimpses of the Cheviot Hills in the west and then the coastal expanses lying to the east.

Beginning from the centre of Rothbury you've first got a steep climb up to Sharpe's Folly. Follies are ornamental structures which have no purpose at all beside enhancing the landscape, and this one is Northumberland's oldest. From here, you'll start ticking off the minor crags, including Dove and Old Stell, before reaching Simonside itself, the area's namesake, which rises over the Coquet Valley. I've included a short out-and-back to Tosson Hill so that you can spend a bit more time enjoying the hills, but you can easily skip this section for a shorter walk (it's about 14 kilometres without). Either way, after descending from Simonside you'll follow the river back to Rothbury where you'll find plenty of cafes, pubs and shops.

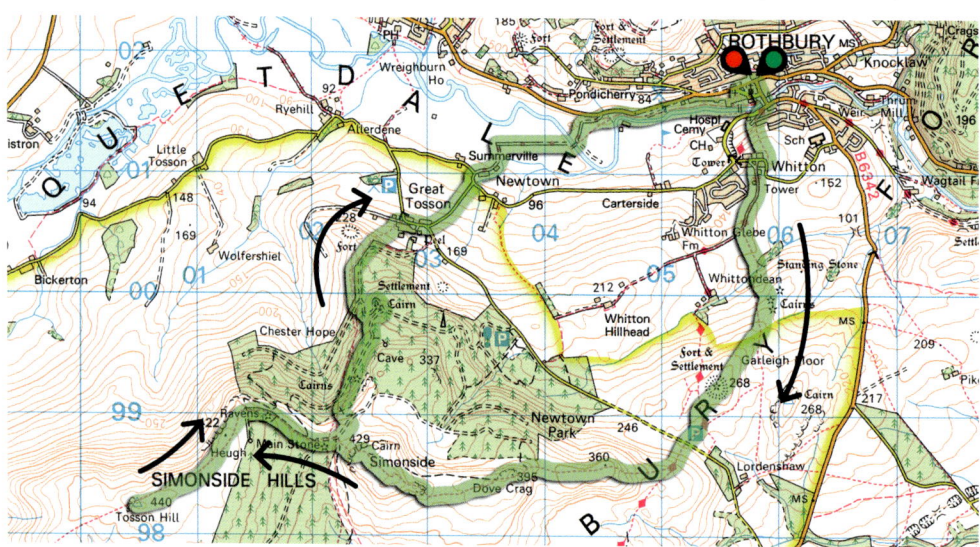

ENGLAND & THE ISLES

1 Bamburgh Castle © Dave Parry

54 Alnmouth to Bamburgh

CATEGORY **Challenge**   DISTANCE **33km**
ASCENT **130m**   START **Alnmouth**
FINISH **Bamburgh**   PUBLIC TRANSPORT **Outbound: bus to Alnmouth (15 minutes). Return: bus from Bamburgh (1 hour 15 minutes).**

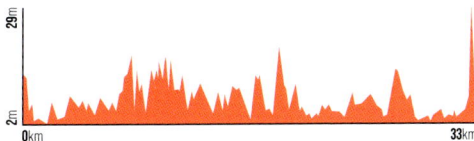

Making use of local buses allows you to tackle a linear section of the Northumberland Coast Path, meaning you can explore more without having to retrace your steps. On this 33-kilometre stretch between Alnmouth and Bamburgh you'll be able to tick off some of Northumberland's most famous sights and soak in a good dose of 'vitamin sea'. Don't worry if you don't fancy the full distance in one go; the bus follows the coast so you can easily split it up into more manageable chunks.

This coastal trail is simple navigationally. All you need to do is keep the sea to your right and focus on enjoying the views. The hardest part might be keeping moving, especially on a warm day, with so many delightful beaches tempting you to have a sit down. It's worth keeping going though, as eventually you'll reach Bamburgh with its iconic castle. Fully restored in the 18th and 19th centuries, the castle is open to the public and a popular tourist attraction. It's a great spot to sit outside and soak in the feeling of history, if you don't fancy a tour.

1 Beadnell Bay © Dave Parry 2 Looking across to the Farne Islands © Helen Parry

55 Northumberland Coast Path

CATEGORY **Multi-day**   DISTANCE **100km**   ASCENT **570m**   START **Cresswell**   FINISH **Berwick-upon-Tweed**
PUBLIC TRANSPORT **Outbound: train to Newcastle or Alnmouth then bus to Ellington (3km from Cresswell). Return: train from Berwick-upon-Tweed.**   MORE INFORMATION **www.northumberlandcoastpath.org**

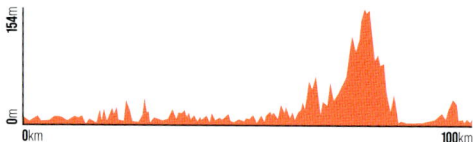

You'll have become fairly well acquainted with many sections of the Northumberland Coast Path over the course of this section already. If you've liked the sound of these shorter stretches, then I strongly urge you to consider having a go at the whole Northumberland Coast Path. It's absolutely stunning from start to finish, with huge sweeping beaches, some of the best seawater quality in the country, castle ruins to wander past and imagine times gone by, several nature reserves and dramatic rocky headlands.

The Northumberland Coast Path is 100 kilometres long and is relatively flat, mostly following pretty good tracks. Typically completed in six stages, this makes for a great week-long holiday equally rich with historical significance and natural beauty.

If you liked this
For a similarly tranquil coastline, head to the Moray Firth in north-east Scotland, which is easily reached by train to Elgin then local buses from there. As well as beautiful beaches, Moray is known for playing host to a pod of 200 bottlenose dolphins, as well as being a good place to see harbour porpoises and whales. The Moray Coast Trail runs for 72 kilometres if you fancy a big adventure around this area.

WALES

Pembrokeshire 107
56 Porthclais Harbour Loop 108
57 Solva to St Davids 109
58 St Davids to Trefin 110
59 St Davids Peninsula 112
60 Pembrokeshire Coast Path 114

Bannau Brycheiniog/Brecon Beacons 117
61 Ysgyryd Fach/Little Skirrid 118
62 Blorenge and Keeper's Pond 119
63 Pen Allt-mawr and Table Mountain 120
64 Abergavenny Three Peaks 122
65 Beacons Way 124

Eryri/Snowdonia 127
66 Chwarel Dinorwig 128
67 Llyn Padarn Loop 129
68 Yr Wyddfa/Snowdon 130
69 Tryfan and the Glyderau 132
70 Llwybr Llechi Eryri/Snowdonia Slate Trail 133

Opposite Pembrokeshire Coast Path

Pembrokeshire

BASE LOCATION **St Davids/Tyddewi**

WHERE TO STAY **Range of self-catering options and B&Bs in St Davids. YHA St Davids is 4km from St Davids. Multiple campsites within walking distance.**

HOW TO GET THERE **Bus to St Davids from train connections in Haverfordwest (direct from Cardiff with onward connections from there)**

There's something special about Pembrokeshire. Tucked away in the south-west corner of Wales, this national park's official tagline is 'A wonder filled coast,' and it's hard to disagree with that description. Yet it's a place I sometimes forget about, perhaps because its location can make it a bit of a slog to get to from many other areas of the country – but it's worth any effort a hundred times over.

With around 420 kilometres of dramatic coastline, Pembrokeshire is home to a seemingly endless supply of hidden coves, enough clifftop trails to keep you occupied for weeks and plenty of picturesque villages full of pubs and cafes to keep you going along the way. This is one for wildlife lovers too, with the opportunity to see many native species that have vanished from other areas of the UK. Make sure your binoculars are close by at all times and keep an eye out for rare birds like choughs and skylarks.

I've chosen Britain's smallest city (by population), St Davids, as the base location for this chapter. Don't let the word 'city' put you off though – nestled within the peninsula of the same name and with access to unspoilt coastal heathland in all directions, St Davids feels more like a village. You'll find numerous routes on your doorstep if you choose to stay here, from circular loops around postcard-worthy harbours to epic point-to-point routes making use of the local bus services.

I stayed at Caerfai Farm Campsite which, along with sea-view pitches and an on-site farm shop and bakery, also offers a discount to anybody arriving by public transport or by bike.

1 Pembrokeshire Coast Path **2** Porthclais Harbour **3** Puffins on Skomer Island
4 Stack Rocks **5** St Davids Cathedral **6** National Trail signs

56 Porthclais Harbour Loop

CATEGORY **Short**   DISTANCE **5km**
ASCENT **80m**   START/FINISH **St Davids**

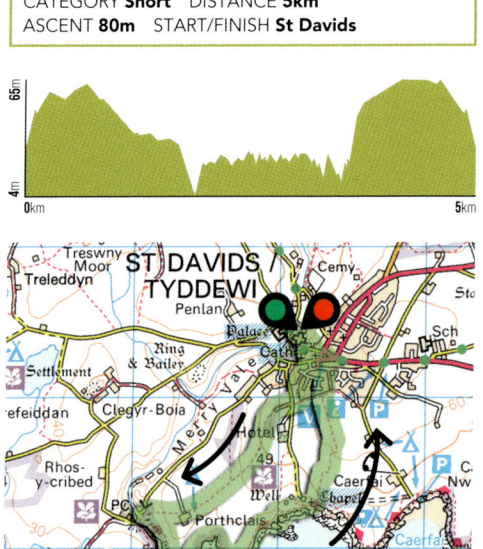

Starting from the cathedral which gives St Davids its city status, this loop packs a punch far greater than its length and feels as though it gives you a taste of everything the peninsula has to offer. A well-kept track takes you away from the crowds and down to Porthclais Harbour where, if you had visited 900 years ago, you would have found a bustling port. Today you'll just find a sleepy harbour popular with kayakers, with small boats bobbing around in the – at times – almost startlingly turquoise water. The former pump room is now home to a kiosk serving a locally sourced menu (ice creams, most importantly, if you do this on a day that's anywhere near as warm as when I did it, or hot soup if you're less lucky).

Heading east from the harbour, you'll follow the coastline past the historic ruins of St Non's Chapel before turning inland. If you fancy a swim, you can continue on a little further to Caerfai Bay and then walk up the lane from there to return to town.

57 Solva to St Davids

CATEGORY **Medium**   DISTANCE **9km**   ASCENT **140m**   START **Solva**   FINISH **St Davids**   PUBLIC TRANSPORT **Outbound: bus to Solva (15 minutes)**

Don't just take my word for it about this route. It claims the lofty honour of having been voted sixteenth in a 2017 ITV poll to find Britain's favourite walk (something I only found out having already chosen to include it in this book – great minds and all). It's easy to see why though – as well as taking you along a beautiful stretch of coastline you'll also be following in historic footsteps as this route once formed the last section of an important medieval pilgrimage. Along the way you'll be able to tick off a number of holy artefacts (a stone circle and coastal fort, Celtic crosses and chapels, along with some holy wells) before finishing at the stunning St Davids Cathedral.

Let's not get ahead of ourselves though. After a morning in St Davids holed up in the aptly named Pilgrims Cafe (worth a visit for their build-your-own breakfast baps) dodging some torrential rain, I eventually hopped on the bus mid-afternoon for the short journey to Solva to begin this route. It's worth taking a wander down Solva's High Street before you start your journey back to St Davids as, for a small village, it's absolutely packed with cafes, restaurants, art galleries and independent shops. You'll then pick up the coast path from the impressive harbour and head westward. While the rain had eased off by this point when I was there, the wind was still high which made for a fairly invigorating experience (and I nearly lost my hat a few times) but in some ways that only amplified the frankly biblical feel of this rugged coast.

If it works better with the bus timetables, you could also do this route in reverse and catch the bus back at the end. Or for a longer walk, stay on the bus for a few more stops to Newgale and start your walk there instead, which gives you an extra 7 kilometres of coast path to enjoy.

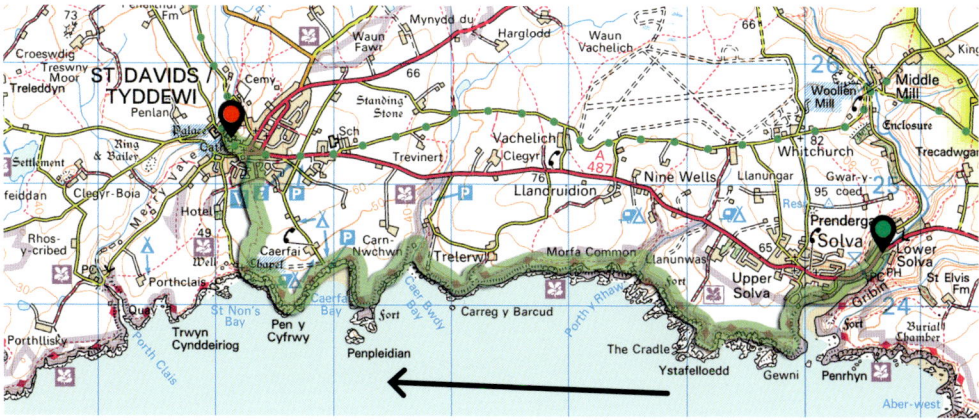

1 Aberfelin Corn Mill/Melin Trefin © jimmonkphotography/Shutterstock.com
2 The Blue Lagoon © Helen Hotson/Shutterstock.com

58 St Davids to Trefin

CATEGORY **Long**   DISTANCE **20km**
ASCENT **320m**   START **St Davids**   FINISH **Trefin**
PUBLIC TRANSPORT **Return: bus from Trefin to St Davids (25 minutes)**

This point-to-point route begins by following the same lanes out of St Davids as in route 59 then heading east once you reach the coast. You'll pass Carn Llidi on the way, which is actually one of several tors made from igneous rock. Another one to keep an eye out for is Carn Penberry, a few kilometres in. Seventy million years ago these were islands; today they give you a chance to see whole swathes of Pembrokeshire and beyond laid out before you on a clear day.

This coastal route is simple enough in theory but contains some steep climbs and rocky terrain keeping things interesting (as well as a few inlets to navigate). There's plenty to see along the way too, as well as the coastal views which you start taking for granted after a couple of days in Pembrokeshire. With everything from natural water features to historical landmarks to explore, make sure you set off early enough to allow for stops. One Komoot user created a highlight for this route simply called 'nice' and I'm not sure I can sum it up better myself.

The Blue Lagoon in Abereiddy is especially worth a visit; it is around 25 metres deep and surrounded by old engine house workings to jump from if you're brave enough. It does get busy though – I visited on a sunny Saturday at the beginning of the school holidays, which was probably a mistake although made for a fun atmosphere. Potentially better saved for the quieter months unless you're in the market for the festival vibes. Industrial history follows you the whole way to Trefin too, as you pass a series of eerie abandoned mining buildings and Victorian brickwork remains. Just before Trefin, you pass the ruins of Aberfelin Corn Mill made famous by Crwys's poem *Melin Trefin*.

Trefin is a small village, but the 240-year-old Ship Inn gives you the perfect place to wait for your next bus. Or, if you happen to be there when it's open, check out the Trefin Museum.

1 Ponies on St Davids Head **2–3** Carn Llidi

59 St Davids Peninsula

CATEGORY **Long**   DISTANCE **21km**
ASCENT **270m**   START/FINISH **St Davids**

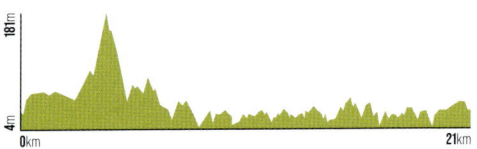

I kind of went off coast paths for a few years. Perhaps I shouldn't admit this while encouraging you to go and visit several coastal locations, but I guess honesty is the best policy. With a new-found obsession with mountains and high places, I just hadn't really felt that excited by the coast.

But this route changed that. Genuinely! Things got off to a good start when I woke up on Caerfai Farm Campsite to a view of the sea. I ate some cereal and then felt so excited by the fact that it wasn't raining that I sat around drinking Jetboiled coffee until 11 a.m., when I finally chucked some snacks and waterproofs (just in case) in a bag and set off on this loop. It was a delight, an absolute delight. Along the way I listened to a podcast about orcas and just felt very 'at one' with the sea.

If your day goes anything like mine, first you'll follow some quiet country lanes out of St Davids and up to the northern side of the peninsula, then you'll head up Carn Llidi. This ascent is optional (you could skirt around it to the east) but it's worth heading up the rocky hill for a good vantage point over the route you have come up. Looking west you'll see exactly where you're heading next, around St Davids Head (Penmaen Dewi) and along the coast stretching from there. Views soaked in, you'll enjoy the downhill from Carn Llidi before crossing a patch of heathery moorland and picking up the coast path.

The work of the Pembrokeshire Grazing Network project means that you're likely to see Welsh mountain ponies enjoying this area of the coast too. The scheme is the longest running of its kind – since 1999 it has been reintroducing traditional farming practices like pony grazing in order to conserve coastal wildlife. Fantastic both for the environment and for your views! I recommend stopping to enjoy a snack somewhere around St Davids Head to take all of this in. (I went for a flapjack, in case you need some inspiration.)

Following the coast path for the next 12 kilometres means you can relax and not worry too much about navigation. For a big chunk of this you'll be able to see over to Ramsey Island, an RSPB reserve lying a kilometre offshore. For a bonus activity, arrange a boat trip to Ramsey from St Justinian's and explore the 6-kilometre trail around the island. In the spring this is a bird lover's dream with many species coming to nest, while in the autumn several hundred seal pups are born on Ramsey's coastline.

Turning your back on Ramsey, the trail continues to traverse the cliffs before heading inland at Porthclais Harbour, which personally I think you get the best view of from this direction. Stop here for a well-deserved ice cream before picking up the trail back into St Davids. If you've packed your swimming costume, then your best bets for a dip come earlier in the day, either at Whitesands Bay (where you'll also find toilets and a drinking water tap) or Porthselau Beach. If you're having too nice a time to stop, then continue on from Porthclais around to Caerfai Bay and go for a swim here (adding an extra 3 kilometres to the route).

WALK BRITAIN

1 Coast path between Newgale and Solva 2 Wales Coast Path signs
3 Pembrokeshire Coast Path trails 4 Porthmynawyd beach

60 Pembrokeshire Coast Path

CATEGORY **Multi-day**   DISTANCE **299km**   ASCENT **4,090m**   START **St Dogmaels (near Cardigan)**
FINISH **Amroth**   PUBLIC TRANSPORT **Outbound: train to Carmarthen or Aberystwyth, then bus to Cardigan. Return: bus to Kilgetty, Tenby or Carmarthen then train connections from there.**   MORE INFORMATION **www.nationaltrail.co.uk**

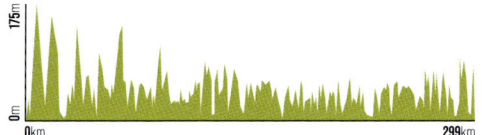

Hopefully these routes have given you a taste of how incredible Pembrokeshire is. Perched on the very western edge of our island and unspoiled in so many ways, including it in this book was non-negotiable for me. The tricky thing was finding an area you could easily access by public transport as sadly that's not the case for large parts of the county, where the remoteness which makes it special also makes it somewhat inaccessible without a car.

The best solution I can think of if you want to explore more of Pembrokeshire is to challenge yourself to do the whole Pembrokeshire Coast Path, where your own legs will prove your most reliable form of transport. At 299 kilometres in length, this designated National Trail will transport you from St Dogmaels in the north to Amroth in the south, with days' worth of coastal adventures waiting for you between the two.

If you liked this
Truly one of the best days out I've ever had was in Pembrokeshire – my destination was Skomer Island, where more than 40,000 puffins migrate every year between April and July. I'm not a bird person but I was absolutely blown away by being in such close proximity to the puffins. Approximately 50 per cent of my camera roll is still just pictures of puffins. To visit Skomer, you need to pre-book a boat trip at *www.pembrokeshire-islands.co.uk* Boats go from Martin's Haven on the Dale Peninsula and, I won't lie, this is a bit of a faff to get to via public transport but I hope you'll agree it's worth it once you get there. Your best bet is to take the train to Haverfordwest then use the local on-demand bus service (bookable at *www.fflecsi.wales*). Or, if you're staying in St Davids in the summer, there is a bus service to Martin's Haven (the Puffin Shuttle, see *www.pembrokeshire.gov.uk/bus-routes-and-timetables*).

Bannau Brycheiniog/ Brecon Beacons

BASE LOCATION **Abergavenny/Y Fenni**

WHERE TO STAY **Range of self-catering options, B&Bs and hotels in Abergavenny. Campsite at Pyscodlyn Farm (15 minutes from Abergavenny by bus).**

HOW TO GET THERE **Trains to Abergavenny**

When I moved to Bristol in 2019, one of the main things I was excited about was being so close to the Brecon Beacons. I had researched the journey there before I'd even thought about finding a new job or flat hunting or anything sensible like that. Coming from London, I was enthralled by the prospect of being able to get on a train and be in the hills just over an hour later. I lived in Bristol for three years in the end and this novelty never really wore off.

The Brecon Beacons National Park covers over 1,300 square kilometres of mountainous ground, hovering on the border between south and mid Wales. The easiest place to explore from using public transport is Abergavenny, which sits between the Black Mountains (the north-eastern part of the national park) and the central Brecon Beacons. With the River Usk flowing through, the market town makes for a great base as it has good national rail connections, several fantastic routes you can do directly from the town and buses to connect you to the peaks further afield.

You'll notice the absence of Pen y Fan in this chapter – one of Wales's most popular walks and the tallest peak in the south of the country – and this is for a couple of reasons. Firstly, I think that Pen y Fan gets enough visitors and probably doesn't need my help promoting it. Secondly, and most importantly, it's not super easy to access without a car. However, if you are keen to tick this one off (admittedly a Welsh walkers' rite of passage), then you can take the train to Cardiff then hop on the bus to the Storey Arms from there. My advice would be to avoid this honeypot and see what else the Brecon Beacons has to offer instead.

1 Backpacking in the Brecon Beacons **2** Coffee break on Pen Allt-mawr **3** Ysgyryd Fawr
4 Snowy Blorenge **5** Table Mountain **6** Blorenge

1 Lamb in the Brecon Beacons © Archie Secrett/Shutterstock.com

61 Ysgyryd Fach/Little Skirrid

CATEGORY **Short** DISTANCE **4km** ASCENT **200m**
START/FINISH **Abergavenny**

Ysgyryd Fach (meaning Little Skirrid) is a hill which stands alone just outside of Abergavenny. At 271 metres tall it's only around half the height of its more popular neighbours, Y Fâl (Sugar Loaf) and Ysgyryd Fawr (Big Skirrid), which are both featured in route 64. That's one of the reasons I think this makes such a nice walk though. You'll often find it much quieter, yet the views from the top of Little Skirrid are fantastic, allowing you to see down over Abergavenny and across to those neighbouring peaks. Bigger isn't always better!

Another advantage of Little Skirrid is that it's situated just behind Abergavenny station. Stepping out from the station, you first have to cross over the busy A465 which is admittedly the worst part of the route. But from here you're on to the good stuff. Little Skirrid is almost entirely covered in conifer plantations; the steep wooded ascent leads you to the summit, and to those views over Abergavenny.

Descending on the other side of the hill, you'll then follow farm tracks back to the station. When I did this route, one of the footpaths went through the noisiest field of sheep I've ever heard, so that's something to potentially look forward to.

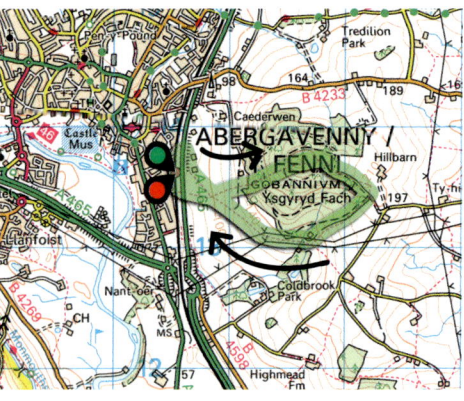

WALES

62 Blorenge and Keeper's Pond

CATEGORY **Medium**   DISTANCE **13km**   ASCENT **520m**   START/FINISH **Llanfoist/Llanffwyst**
PUBLIC TRANSPORT **Both ways: buses between Abergavenny and Llanfoist (15 minutes)**

The most popular route around Blorenge (Blorens in Welsh) involves driving almost to the top and walking a circular route of around 11 kilometres from there. Our car-free option extends the walk slightly, joining up with the classic route by way of a sharp initial climb up through the woods from the bus stop in Llanfoist. It is about a 30-minute walk from the centre of Abergavenny to Llanfoist but you can take a local bus if you want to avoid the extra road miles.

Sitting at 561 metres, Blorenge is a designated Site of Special Scientific Interest thanks to its vast amounts of heather moorland, which provides a home to upland birdlife and many rare species. You'll also walk through the Punchbowl, a glacial cwm with a man-made lake which is one of two wild swimming spots on the route. The second is Keeper's Pond (Pen-ffordd-goch Pond), which you'll reach just before the summit – this has to be one of the most scenic places I've ever taken a dip, perched above the surrounding towns with moorland and mountain views all around. On a clear day you can see across to the higher peaks of the Brecon Beacons from Blorenge – you should be able to spot Pen y Fan, Corn Du and Cribyn.

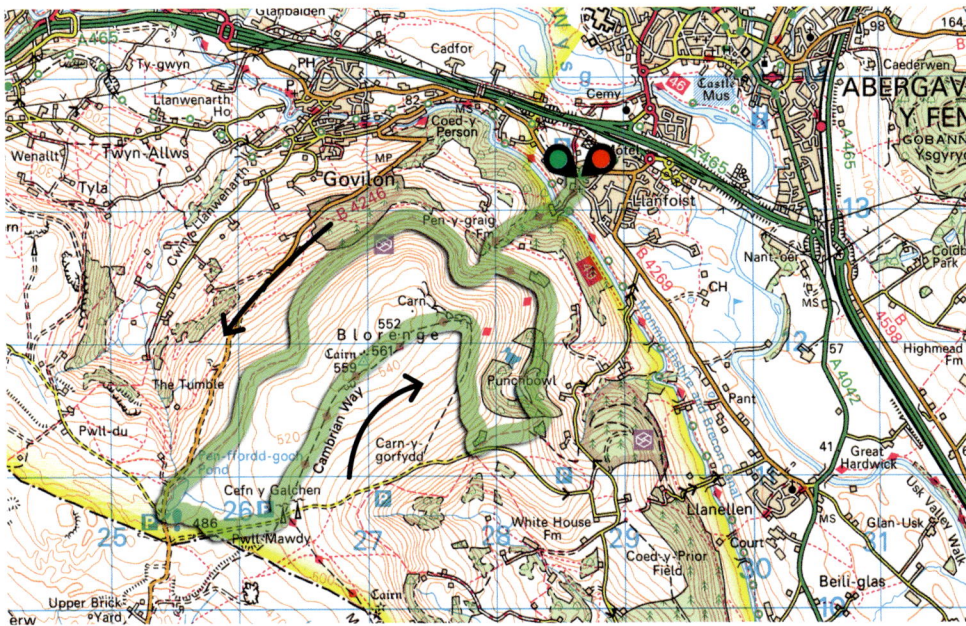

1 Sunset on Pen Allt-mawr 2 Table Mountain 3 Pen Cerrig-calch trig point

63 Pen Allt-mawr and Table Mountain

CATEGORY **Long**   DISTANCE **19km**   ASCENT **790m**
START/FINISH **Crickhowell/Crughywel**
PUBLIC TRANSPORT **Both ways: buses between Abergavenny and Crickhowell (25 minutes)**

In my opinion, Crickhowell is the place to be in the Brecon Beacons. It's a fantastic little village, with a few good pubs (try the Bear Hotel for an open fire, great food and, depending when you visit, excessive amounts of Christmas decor), a craft beer bar which randomly also serves quiche, and several tea rooms, ice cream shops, and so on. I chose Abergavenny for the base location in this chapter for ease of transport and access to several good walking routes, but I'd recommend considering staying in Crickhowell too. Or at least hopping on the bus and visiting for the day to do this route.

Pen Allt-mawr is a subsidiary peak of Waun Fach, but in its own right is the third tallest summit in the Black Mountains, at 719 metres. This route skirts around the bottom flanks of Waun Fach's southern ridge, before climbing up to Pen Allt-mawr and then continuing along to Pen Cerrig-calch. I really recommend this one for an afternoon walk if you get a clear day, timing it so you're heading along this ridge at golden hour. The descent takes you along to the flat-topped Table Mountain. Perhaps not quite as impressive as the mighty South African mountain of the same name but still a very pleasant place to spend sunset.

You'll be fine donning your head torch for the final stretch of the walk, should you manage to correctly time this fantasy weather scenario that I've just conjured up, as you're mainly on good tracks and then the road back into Crickhowell.

1 Blorenge trig point 2–3 Ysgyryd Fawr

64 Abergavenny Three Peaks

CATEGORY **Challenge**   DISTANCE **34km**
ASCENT **1,360m**   START/FINISH **Abergavenny**

There are three main hills surrounding Abergavenny: Blorenge/Blorens (see route 62), Y Fâl (Sugar Loaf) and Ysgyryd Fawr (Big Skirrid). Relatively modest in stature, they may not be the big-ticket hikes that the Brecon Beacons is famous for but they still offer some great walking and running. You could fill a fantastic long weekend by staying in Abergavenny and tackling one per day but, for a bigger challenge, this route allows you to summit them all in one day. My attempts to complete this route in a day were thwarted by the Bailey bridge in Glangrwyney being closed, but thankfully it is now open again after several years of being out of bounds. Handy for residents, I'm sure, but also for Three-Peakers.

Beginning in Abergavenny, you'll first climb Blorenge, before a long lowland section making your way over to Sugar Loaf, following the canal and then some country lanes (and crossing the once-closed bridge). This is the highest summit of the day at 596 metres, known for its distinctive summit. From Sugar Loaf it's on to Big Skirrid, which might be my favourite of the three.

Ysgyryd Fawr is known as the 'Holy Mountain' because, as legend goes, the landslide on the mountain's northern tip was apparently caused by a lightning strike that took place as Christ was crucified. While I can't quite vouch for the accuracy of this dramatic claim, Big Skirrid certainly makes for a good walk. On this loop you'll ascend Ysgyryd Fawr from the north, via a particularly steep climb. You'll emerge on to the summit at the trig point, likely much to the surprise of everybody who came up the gentler way, who'll be wondering why you're panting so hard. This is what happened to me the first time I did it in any case, on day two of an overnight hike with a friend, carrying heavy bags and sweating profusely.

Your reward for taking the hard way up is a leisurely descent along Big Skirrid's ridge with views in all directions. From Big Skirrid's position on the edge of the Black Mountains, you can see from the Malvern Hills in the northeast, round to Somerset in the south and across from the Forest of Dean in the east over to the rest of the Brecon Beacons in the west. It's a landscape worthy of a much bigger hill.

Your last task of the day is to make your way back to Abergavenny. With a solid 34 kilometres and nearly 1,400 metres of climbing in your legs, you'll be well deserving of a good feed at one of Abergavenny's many restaurants. If you're back early enough, my top cafe pick is Bean and Bread.

For even more of a challenge, why not create your own route inspired by the historic Seven Hills of Abergavenny (as detailed in Chris Barber's book of the same name). The peaks are: Blorenge, Llanwenarth, Rholben, Sugar Loaf, Deri, Ysgyryd Fawr and Ysgyryd Fach.

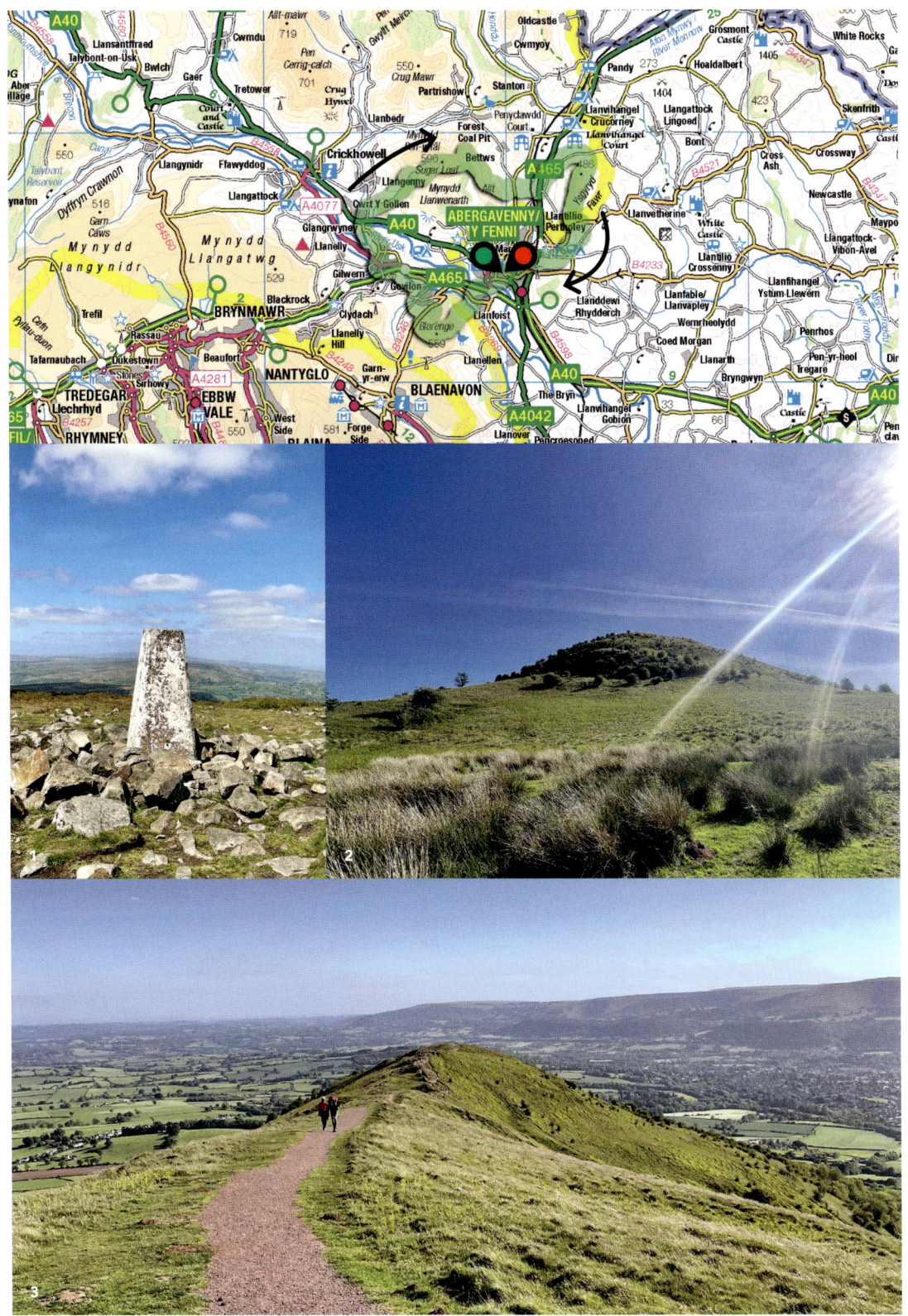

WALK BRITAIN

1 Hiking towards Fan y Big   2 Walking towards Picws Du   Both photos © Becky the Traveller

65 Beacons Way

CATEGORY **Multi-day**   DISTANCE **159km**   ASCENT **5,440m**   START **Abergavenny**   FINISH **Llangadog**
PUBLIC TRANSPORT **Outbound: trains to Abergavenny. Return: trains from Llangadog.**   MORE INFORMATION www.breconbeaconsparksociety.org

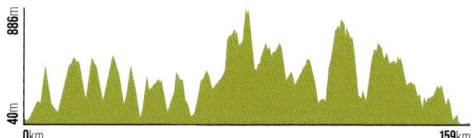

Like several of the other long-distance routes I've included, the Beacons Way serves two purposes. First, it's just a brilliant trail that guarantees you a fantastic backpacking adventure (or at least a memorable one, depending how much that famous Welsh weather comes out to play). Secondly, and specifically for the purposes of this book, it gives you the chance to explore areas of the Brecon Beacons which are otherwise inaccessible without a car. Win–win!

The 159-kilometre route travels east to west, crossing the entire breadth of the national park. Beginning in Abergavenny, you'll travel over rugged high peaks and rounded grassy hills, past crystal clean llyns (lakes) and beside glacial cwms on your way to Llangadog. Typically completed in eight stages of between 16 and 24 kilometres apiece, there are no easy days on this route. But then you don't do long-distance hiking in search of an easy life, do you?

If you liked this
Head to the wild west of the Brecon Beacons for a brilliantly remote adventure. Public transport can be scarse, but one option is to catch the bus to Brynamman from Swansea and explore the hills around there. For something different, another South Wales gem is the Gower Peninsula which is hugged by a beautiful and at times brutal coast path. Take the train to Swansea or Gowerton then use local buses to get you on to the peninsula.

Eryri/Snowdonia

BASE LOCATION **Llanberis**

WHERE TO STAY **Wide range of self-catering options and B&Bs in Llanberis. YHA Snowdon Llanberis and Camping in Llanberis are both a short walk from the centre of the village.**

HOW TO GET THERE **Train to Bangor or Betws-y-Coed then bus to Llanberis**

Yr Wyddfa (Snowdon) was the first mountain I ever climbed. I was six years old and wearing some platform Spice-Girls-style trainers from British Home Stores with gingham cycling shorts and an oversized sweater. Not sure what my parents were thinking but if you went up Snowdon today, you'd probably find quite a few people wearing almost identical outfits, thanks to the resurgence of 90s fashion. I don't like to kit shame, but I'd probably recommend ditching the Sporty Spice trainers in favour of some proper walking footwear.

I'd be lying if I told you I remembered much about that 1998 ascent but more recent trips to Eryri have confirmed it worthy of including in this book. Covering over 2,000 square kilometres, this designated national park in North Wales has a little bit of everything, including nine mountain ranges, 119 kilometres of coastline and 110 square kilometres of native woodland.

From lakeside wanders to ascents of some of England and Wales's highest points, this chapter will focus on the mountain areas that Eryri is so famous for. The outdoors hub of Llanberis is our base location, with its prime setting on the banks of the majestic Llyn Padarn and its many accommodation options, including campsites and a youth hostel.

1 Eryri National Park views **2** Climbing Tryfan **3** Stopping for a rest at one of the many quarries on the Snowdonia Slate Trail © Becky the Traveller **4** Cantilever Stone on Glyder Fach **5** Views from the Miners' Track on Yr Wyddfa

1 Chwarel Dinorwig   2 Llyn Padarn   Both photos © Dave Parry

66 Chwarel Dinorwig

CATEGORY **Short**   DISTANCE **5km**
ASCENT **220m**   START/FINISH **Llanberis**

This huge former slate quarry sits just above Llanberis and is home to the National Slate Museum. Slate forms a huge part of the history in this area, as is clear if you do the Llwybr Llechi Eryri/Snowdonia Slate Trail (route 70). This out-and-back route gives you a chance to experience some of this heritage in a slightly shorter timeframe, with some absolutely magnificent views of Llyn Padarn, Llyn Peris and the surrounding hills too.

You'll be following the main walking path, which snakes through just some of the 700 acres that made up Dinorwig. The highest working level of the old quarry was 670 metres above sea level and although we don't go that high, there's still a steep climb up.

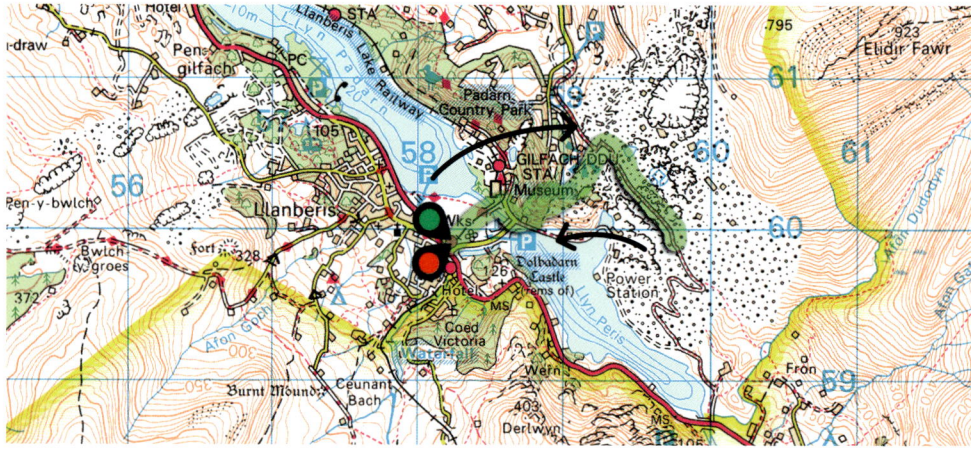

67 Llyn Padarn Loop

CATEGORY **Medium**   DISTANCE **9km**
ASCENT **120m**   START/FINISH **Llanberis**

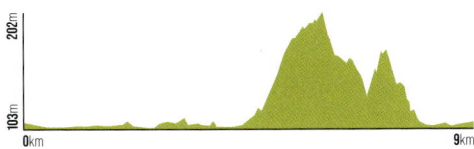

Although there are countless opportunities to get up high in Eryri (with 17 peaks over 900 metres in the area), I always think it's good to have a couple of low-level walks in your back pocket too. Perfect for rainy days when the conditions up top are unappealing at best (and dangerous at worst), when you're short on time or if you're a runner who wants to actually run rather than hike up hills and scramble down them all day. For all those scenarios, this loop around Llyn Padarn from Llanberis is the perfect choice. It's a straightforward route with big pay-off.

The *pièce de résistance* is, of course, Llyn Padarn. This glacially formed lake is 3 kilometres long and, bordered by mountains, it's probably one of the most postcard-worthy spots in this book (especially when you pass the famous Lone Tree around 1.5 kilometres into this walk). It's one of the largest natural lakes in Wales and some rare breeds live beneath its surface, including the Arctic charr fish which is usually found in colder places but became stranded in some British lakes following the last ice age.

This route isn't just about the water though. You also have sections through ancient woodland, a lovely waterfall to look out for and sights of Dolbadarn Castle. There's a small climb on the northern side of the lake in the second part of the walk, which gives you some fantastic vantage points over the lake as well as views to Yr Wyddfa (Snowdon) itself. However, if you do fancy getting better acquainted with the water, pack your swimming gear as there are plenty of good spots for a dip. It's also a popular paddleboarding location – you can hire boards in Llanberis.

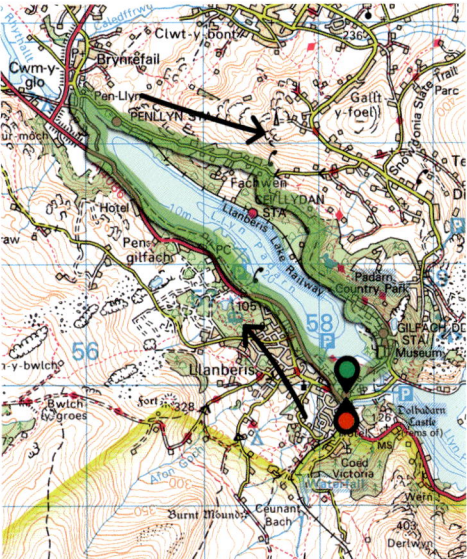

1 Near the summit of Yr Wyddfa © John Coefield

68 Yr Wyddfa/Snowdon

CATEGORY **Long**   DISTANCE **18km**
ASCENT **1,010m**   START/FINISH **Llanberis**

Let's be honest, if we're talking about hidden gems then Yr Wyddfa certainly isn't one – over 600,000 people climb it each year. The sheer volume of visitors does present issues, and I was in two minds about whether to include this route. However, a key issue is the number of cars which descend on the area and all the traffic and related problems caused, so, if you're going to climb Yr Wyddfa, doing it car-free is the way to go.

And I can, of course, understand why you'd want to climb it. It's a tick-list item for many walkers and there's something kind of special about being able to say that, however briefly, you're the highest person in Wales and England. It is also a stunning hike. The views from the top, on a clear day, are hard to beat. I would urge you to consider visiting at off-peak times where you can though, both to balance out the number of visitors and to prevent you having to stand in a queue for the summit. Book a day off work and go midweek if you can. You can get some fantastic days in the spring or autumn, which will likely be quieter than midsummer.

Okay, let's get into the route. There are six main tracks which you can use to climb Yr Wyddfa. This loop takes you up via the Snowdon Ranger Path, which is believed to be the oldest of the six. It's one of the slightly less used tracks, perhaps due to it being a little more challenging underfoot with some sections of loose scree (hence why we're going up this way, rather than down). It's a great chance to explore some of the quieter areas of the Yr Wyddfa massif though. You'll pass Llyn Ffynnon y Gwas on your way up which is a lovely mountain tarn, perfect for a mid-walk cool-off on a sunny day.

From the summit you have two options. The first, as you can see on the map, is to head back down via the Llanberis Path. No matter when you go, you'll likely find it fairly busy on this route, as the relative ease of this track compared to others makes it the most popular choice for summiteers. It's a good path all the way down, so perfect if you don't like descending on unstable terrain. This option also has the advantage of creating a circular route and you'll finish back where you started.

The other option is to follow the Miners' Track down to Pen-y-Pass and then catch the bus back into Llanberis. I like this option as it gives you the chance to descend facing those iconic Yr Wyddfa views, looking over Glaslyn and Llyn Llydaw, and is also generally a little quieter than the Llanberis Path. Just be aware that it is a bit more uneven underfoot on this path.

WALK BRITAIN

1 Tryfan views

69 Tryfan and the Glyderau

CATEGORY **Challenge**   DISTANCE **25km**   ASCENT **1,600m**   START **Llanberis**   FINISH **Capel Curig**
PUBLIC TRANSPORT **Return: bus from Capel Curig (30 minutes)**

Tryfan and the Glyderau is a classic mountain route, thought by many to be one of the best in the country. The typical Tryfan route (starting at Llyn Ogwen) is shorter than the Yr Wyddfa loop (route 68) but more difficult, with lots of scrambling and tricky terrain to challenge yourself on. Your reward for the effort is immense though, with some absolutely spectacular scenery. I was lucky enough to do this route on a perfect summer's day, with barely a cloud in the sky – it's one of my best mountain memories.

You can get to Llyn Ogwen from Llanberis by public transport but it's a bit of faff, involving two buses. To avoid this, I'm suggesting this epic point-to-point route from Llanberis to Capel Curig, which just involves one bus at the end of the day. You'll need some mountain experience for this one but, if you're comfortable on the exposed terrain, it's more than worth the effort.

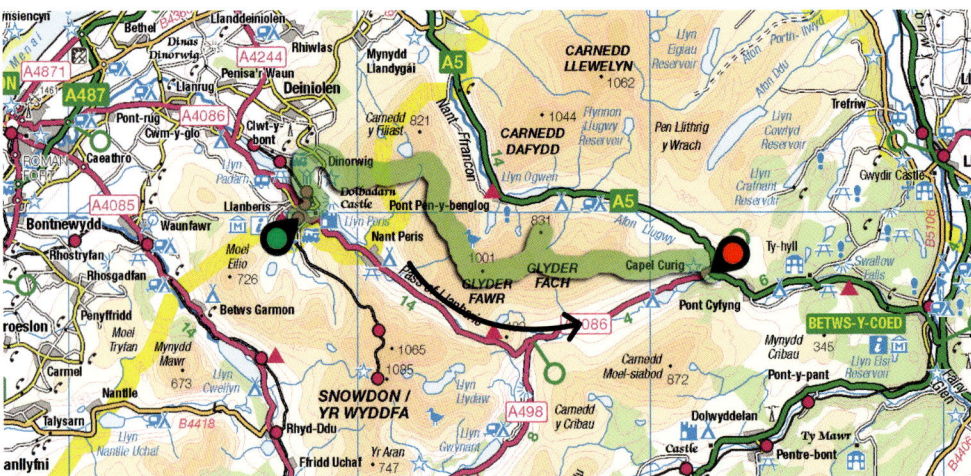

70 Llwybr Llechi Eryri/Snowdonia Slate Trail

CATEGORY **Multi-day**   DISTANCE **136km**   ASCENT **3,340m**   START **Porth Penrhyn, near Bangor**   FINISH **Bethesda**   PUBLIC TRANSPORT **Outbound: train to Bangor. Return: bus to Bangor then rail links from there.**   MORE INFORMATION **www.snowdoniaslatetrail.org**

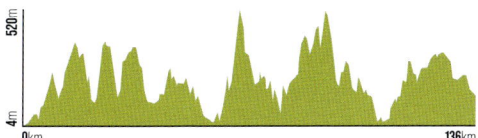

Eryri's slate history began some 500 million years ago when layers of mud became mudstone on an ancient seabed – many millennia later these rocks metamorphosed to become the slate which the area is famous for, some of the best in the world. The Snowdonia Slate Trail is slightly newer, having only been opened in 2017, but is a fantastic asset to the area. This 136-kilometre route starts near Bangor and then sends you off in a big loop around Snowdonia.

There are a few reasons why I think this is such a great trail. Firstly, it passes through all the key mountain ranges of Eryri but stays relatively low down, meaning you get to experience these towering massifs from below. This is similar to the West Highland Way (route 85) and the Cumbria Way (route 45). It's a fantastic way to enjoy these areas and makes these trails *slightly* less weather contingent than high-level routes. Secondly, the Snowdonia Slate Trail takes you through some of the quieter areas of the national park, then contrasts these less-visited villages and less-trodden trails with the major honeypots of Llanberis and Betws-y-Coed. There's something really nice about this balance – peace and quiet and the chance for a chat, all rolled into one.

The route is typically split into seven days, but you can of course combine or divide sections for a slower or faster attempt. The main thing to work out in advance is where you're going to sleep – if you're not camping, you'll be somewhat dictated to by accommodation options, which are sparse in certain areas.

If you liked this

As well as the mountains it's so well known for, Eryri has a superb coastline. The Cambrian Coast Line allows you to explore it easily by train; it hugs the coast all the way from Dovey Junction on the southern Eryri border up to Porthmadog. Many stops are request only, which adds a certain charm. From Porthmadog you can continue on the railway line and venture into the phenomenal Llŷn Peninsula, referred to as the 'Arm of Eryri' and known for its standout beaches.

SCOTLAND

Scottish Borders 137
71 River Tweed and Melrose Abbey 138
72 Eildon Hills Circular 139
73 Galashiels and Yair Hill Forest 140
74 Melrose to Ancrum 141
75 Borders Abbeys Way 142

Isle of Arran 145
76 Brodick Castle 146
77 Loch Tanna 147
78 Sannox to Lochranza 148
79 Goatfell and Glen Rosa 150
80 Arran Coastal Way 152

Western Highlands 155
81 Cow Hill 156
82 Loch Ossian 158
83 Devil's Ridge and the Mamores 160
84 Ben Nevis via the Càrn Mòr Dearg Arête 162
85 West Highland Way 164

Cairngorms 167
86 Aviemore and the River Spey 168
87 Creag Bheag and the Caledonian Pinewoods 169
88 Cairn Gorm and Ben Macdui 170
89 Cairn Toul and Braeriach Traverse 172
90 East Highland Way 174

Opposite Cairngorms National Park

Scottish Borders

> **BASE LOCATION** Melrose
>
> **WHERE TO STAY** A range of self-catering accommodation and B&Bs in Melrose. Camping available at Melrose Gibson Park Club Campsite.
>
> **HOW TO GET THERE** Bus to Melrose from train connections in nearby Tweedbank

The Scottish Borders are a highly underrated area of Great Britain, in my opinion. I visited for the first time when I was meeting a friend who lived a little further north in Scotland, and we randomly picked a spot in the Borders as a good halfway point to have lunch together. As I got closer to our meeting point, I couldn't believe how beautiful the landscape that I was driving through was. All I could think was: why have I never been here before?

But therein lies the problem: the landscape I was *driving* through. I wasn't sure how easy this area would be to access via public transport, but I needn't have worried thanks to the Borders Railway. Opened in 2015, it is the longest new domestic railway to be built in over 100 years and connects Edinburgh and Tweedbank. This incredibly scenic route takes you away from the hustle and bustle of Scotland's capital and right into the heart of the Borders, ready for an adventure.

The train only goes as far as Tweedbank but from here it's only a few minutes on the bus to the lovely town of Melrose. As well as the abbey which dominates the town, you also have the River Tweed and the Eildon Hills to explore. We'll be making use of some more local buses too, so you can venture further afield. Wherever you decide to walk, I recommend spending some time looking around Melrose too. Simply Delicious will serve you a home-made ice cream (it does what it says on the tin) and Abbey Fine Wines has some seating outside which makes for a nice people-watching spot over a drink.

1 Eildon Hills trig point **2** Simply Delicious ice cream in Melrose **3** River Tweed
4 Melrose Abbey © Heartland Arts/Shutterstock.com **5** Eildon Hills viewpoint **6** Bridge over the River Tweed

WALK BRITAIN

1 River Tweed 2 Eildon Hills ascent

71 River Tweed and Melrose Abbey

CATEGORY **Short**   DISTANCE **6km**
ASCENT **50m**   START/FINISH **Melrose**

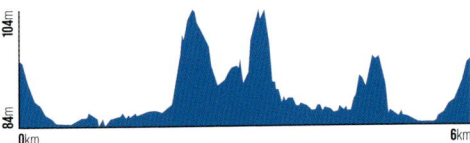

The River Tweed is over 150 kilometres long and flows east all the way through the Scottish Borders to Northern England, where it joins the Berwickshire coast. Tweed cloth got its name from the high number of mills which were powered by the river, which today is one of Europe's greatest salmon rivers. Reportedly plans are underway to create a new long-distance hiking route following the course of the Tweed, but there are various sections where you can already enjoy walking beside the water, like on this loop starting in Melrose.

Starting in the town centre, you'll first pass Melrose Abbey. This partly ruined monastery dates back to the 12th century and it's worth having a look around; the outside is decorated by various unusual sculptures (including but not limited to a bagpipe-playing pig). You then wander down a lane, cross a bridge and pick up the riverside trail. There are a few sections on the road but it's worth it for the time you get to spend by the river, which looks absolutely glorious on a sunny afternoon with the light reflecting off the glass-like water.

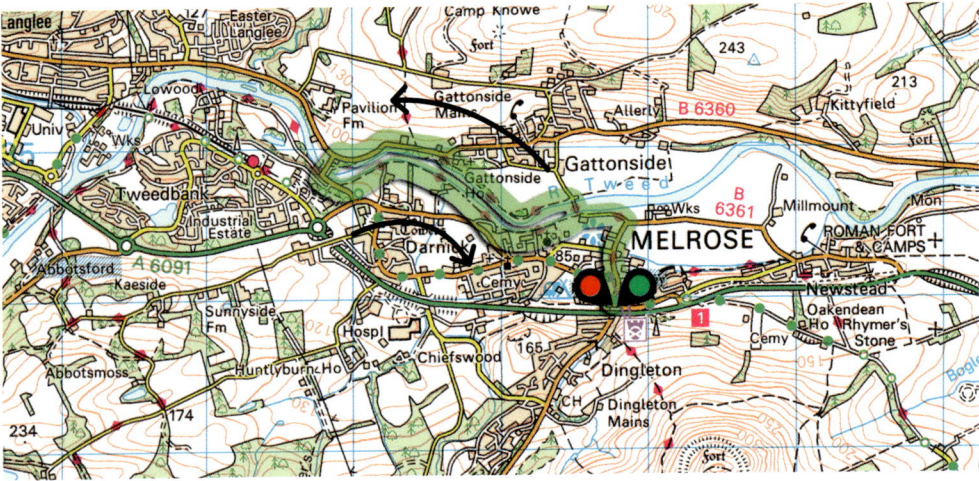

72 Eildon Hills Circular

CATEGORY **Medium**   DISTANCE **9km**
ASCENT **390m**   START/FINISH **Melrose**

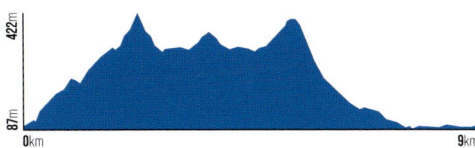

The Eildon Hills are a distinctive feature of the landscape in this area – you can see them from many directions as you approach Melrose. The trio of summits – Eildon Mid Hill, Eildon Wester Hill and Eildon Hill North – are the remainder of an underground volcanic eruption and they really stand out compared to the rest of the Borders landscape, where you'll more commonly find rolling hills.

You follow St Cuthbert's Way for a little while out of Melrose, veering off to follow our route up to each hill. Your first summit is Eildon Mid Hill; you'll know you're there when you not only find a trig point but also a handy view indicator. On a clear day, it's fun to try and spot surrounding sights and on a less clear day you can use your imagination as to what it might be pointing at. Next, it's on to Wester and North hills, the latter being the site of Scotland's largest hillfort during the Iron Age.

I really enjoyed this walk; you get some wonderful views over Melrose and Galashiels from the top, and the feeling of being on much higher ground. There are some steep sections, so make sure you've allowed plenty of time to get around. The route is slightly unintuitive in places and occasionally requires retracing your steps, so make sure you're keeping an eye on the map or your GPS device as the criss-crossing paths can make it confusing.

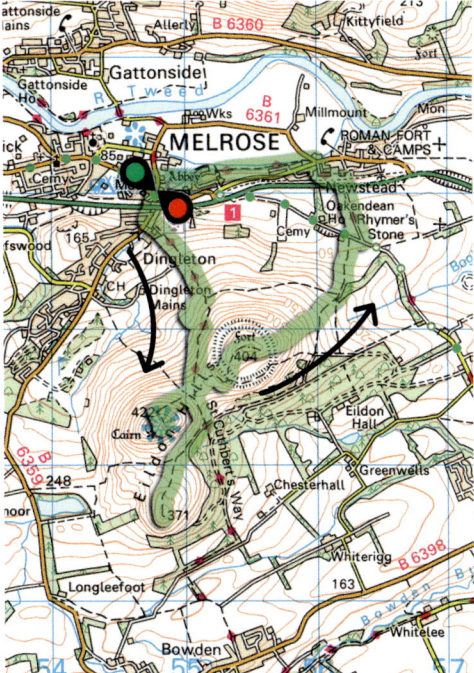

WALK BRITAIN

1 The Three Brethren © Anthony Ackers/Shutterstock.com

73 Galashiels and Yair Hill Forest

CATEGORY **Long** DISTANCE **23km**
ASCENT **870m** START/FINISH **Galashiels**
PUBLIC TRANSPORT **Both ways: buses between Melrose and Galashiels (25 minutes)**

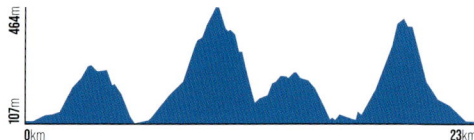

Galashiels is only a short bus journey from Melrose and heading here will give you a chance to explore even more of this area. Although Galashiels is the biggest town in the Borders, you don't have to go far to feel fully immersed in the countryside. This undulating walk is 23 kilometres long but there are a few places where you can shorten it if required.

Taking you across fields, through woodland and up hills, perhaps the biggest appeal of this route are the numerous spots where you can experience panoramic views over the surrounding area. Once in Yair Hill Forest, the Three Brethren are a particular highlight, with some people considering them to offer the best view in the whole of the Scottish Borders. This trio of enormous cairns are said to have stood since the 16th century and from here you'll be able to see the Eildon Hills, which you may have already climbed (see route 72), as well as glimpses of Ettrick Forest's hills.

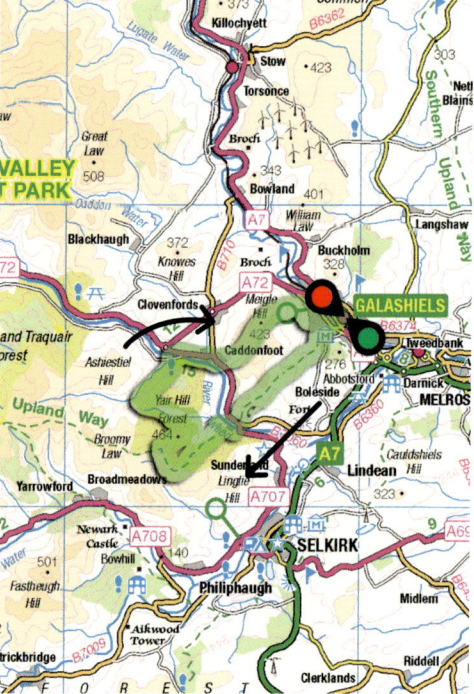

140

SCOTLAND

74 Melrose to Ancrum

CATEGORY **Challenge** DISTANCE **26km** ASCENT **440m** START **Melrose** FINISH **Ancrum**
PUBLIC TRANSPORT **Return: bus from Ancrum (30 minutes)** MORE INFORMATION **www.stcuthbertsway.info, www.scotlandsgreattrails.com**

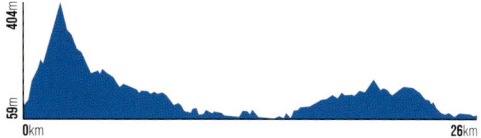

St Cuthbert's Way is a 100-kilometre point-to-point trail which you'll have already become acquainted with if you've done the Eildon Hills Circular (route 72). Running between Melrose and Lindisfarne (Holy Island) on the east coast of England, this trail is named after a 7th-century saint and links places he's thought to have frequented on his pilgrimages. This is the first stage of the trail, a 22-kilometre stretch which ends near Harestanes (from where you can walk on to Ancrum and catch the bus back to Melrose). Our route is a little longer because of the extra section at the end and some short detours to see interesting things along the route.

It's a day out that feels steeped in history from the very start, as you set off from the shadows of Melrose Abbey. The first portion of the day takes you over the saddle between Eildon Hill North and Eildon Mid Hill; from here you can see ahead to the Cheviots (which you explore more if you carry on to do the full St Cuthbert's Way). If you haven't climbed Eildon Hill North before, it's worth the slight detour to visit the Iron Age hillfort at the top.

Descending from the saddle, the rest of your journey will take you over moorland, through native woodland, past churches with hundreds of years of history (make sure you stop at Bowden Kirk), along the banks of the River Tweed and down quiet country lanes. Eventually you'll reach Harestanes Countryside Visitor Centre where you can grab a cup of tea before walking on to Ancrum and hopping on the bus back to Melrose. Or carrying on all the way to the sea, if you like!

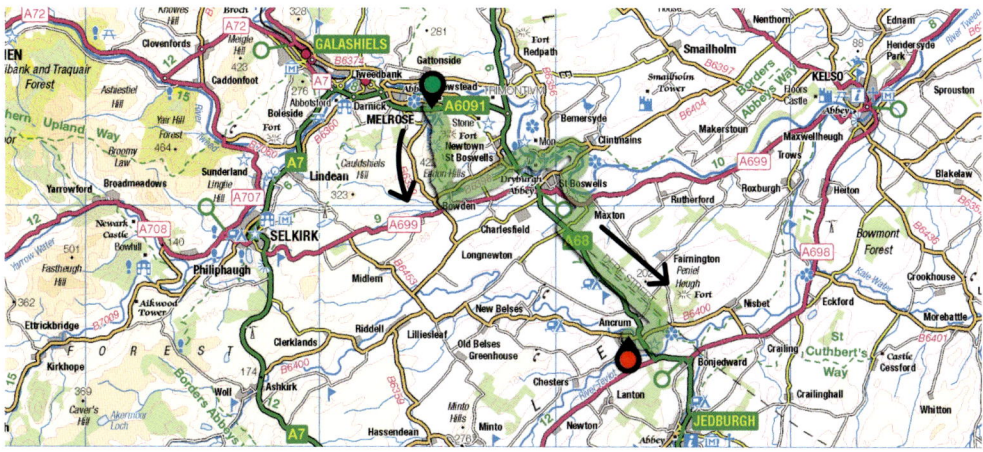

1 Section of the route shared with St Cuthbert's Way **2** Dryburgh Abbey
3 River Teviot in summer **4** Well-signed trails through farmland All photos © Clare Russell

75 Borders Abbeys Way

CATEGORY **Multi-day** DISTANCE **108km** ASCENT **1,440m** START/FINISH **Anywhere on the route – Melrose (near Tweedbank) offers the best transport links** PUBLIC TRANSPORT **Both ways: trains to Tweedbank** MORE INFORMATION **www.scotborders.gov.uk, www.scotlandsgreattrails.com**

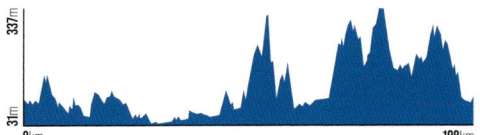

One of Scotland's Great Trails, the Borders Abbeys Way is a circular route which links four of Britain's most impressive ruined medieval abbeys, all of which are located in this part of the Scottish Borders. Over the course of a 108-kilometre loop, you'll take in Melrose, Dryburgh, Kelso and Jedburgh abbeys via a series of forestry tracks, open moorland and riverside paths. Typically beginning and ending in Melrose (although in theory you can start and finish anywhere, this is convenient for the train station at Tweedbank), most people will complete the route over five or six days.

As long-distance trails go, this one is relatively tame. You have under 1,500 metres of climbing over the whole 108 kilometres and you've mostly got good terrain underfoot. There are some more rugged sections to balance out the gentle riverside stretches though and there's a certain amount of pastoral charm to be absorbed as you pass through sleepy villages and farmland. While there's no doubt that this is the perfect trail for history lovers, you won't be disappointed if you're looking for wildlife. You've got a good chance of being joined by buzzards, tortoiseshell butterflies and brown hares on your journey.

If you liked this
Another great spot to explore from in the Scottish Borders is Peebles. Peebles combines outdoorsy appeal with a flourishing arts scene (including a writers' festival and a film festival). Travel there from Edinburgh (1 hour and 15 minutes on the bus). For other ideas near Edinburgh, you can also check out the Pentland Hills, a small range just outside the city. The bus to Balerno takes around 40 minutes from the centre of Edinburgh, and then you can head into the hills from there.

Isle of Arran

BASE LOCATION **Brodick or Lochranza**

WHERE TO STAY **A wide range of self-catering options and B&Bs in Brodick. For hostel and campsite accommodation, try Lochranza.**

HOW TO GET THERE **CalMac ferry from Ardrossan to Brodick. Direct trains from Glasgow to Ardrossan Harbour station take less than 1 hour. Once on Arran, use local buses.**

Often referred to as Scotland in miniature, Arran is one of Scotland's more southerly islands. This means you can get all of that Highland feel and a real sense of wilderness, but with much easier access travelling from the south. In my mind, Arran has it all: coast paths, mountains and truly exceptional sandwiches.

You'll find plenty of information about the trails and the peaks over the following pages, so I'm going to focus on the sandwiches here. Skip this paragraph if you're not as passionate about delicious things between bread as I am. Perched unassumingly over the road from the bus stop in Lochranza, the Sandwich Station claims to be 'Redefining what it means to have a sandwich'. Forget your soggy cheese sandwiches and instead treat yourself to something from the changing daily menu of local ingredients. Goods in hand, the optimal sandwich eating spot is just over the road, where you can find benches and swings looking out to sea. This comes highly recommended as lunch after doing route 78, which finishes in Lochranza, but is worth a trip in its own right.

Okay, back to the adventures. I've tried to show a bit of everything that Arran has to offer in these routes, from coastal trails to ridgeline scrambles and historic sites to remote mountain lochs. As a relatively small island (just 32 kilometres in length), there are fewer options for getting the big miles in, so I've included two medium routes and foregone a challenge option. If you do want to go longer, then your best bet is to try ticking off a chunk of the Arran Coastal Way (route 80).

There's a good bus network circumnavigating the whole island, so you can easily get to the start and end point of the routes. Brodick is the largest village (and where the ferry from the mainland arrives), making it a good base with plenty of choice for accommodation and eating, plus a supermarket. There's plenty going on in Lochranza too though; as well as sandwiches, you'll also find a hostel, campsite, whisky distillery and community-owned pub.

1 Glen Catacol **2** Brodick Bay **3** Chips in Brodick **4** North Goatfell **5** Goatfell summit **6** Loch na Davie

WALK BRITAIN

1 Fisherman's Walk, Brodick   2 Glen Catacol

76 Brodick Castle

CATEGORY **Short**   DISTANCE **7km**   ASCENT **10m**   START/FINISH **Brodick**   PUBLIC TRANSPORT
Both ways: bus to/from Brodick, if needed

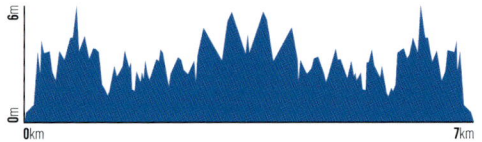

The ferry over from Ardrossan brings you into Brodick Bay, meaning this is the first part of the island you'll see. This shorter walk makes for an ideal leg-stretcher after getting off the ferry. Heading north along the promenade out of Brodick, you soon pick up the Fisherman's Walk boardwalk which will carry you over the marshes. This is the perfect place for birdwatching, as you'll travel through a variety of habitats in a short period (check out *www.arranbirding.co.uk* for more info on which species to look out for).

A left turn takes you away from the coast and leads you to Brodick Castle, Garden and Country Park. You can either retrace your steps back from here, or head into the park (there is an entry fee) to explore its woodland, waterfalls and, of course, the castle. Check out Cladach Beach House on your way back – this beach bar leans into the weather with Alpine ski lodge vibes in the winter.

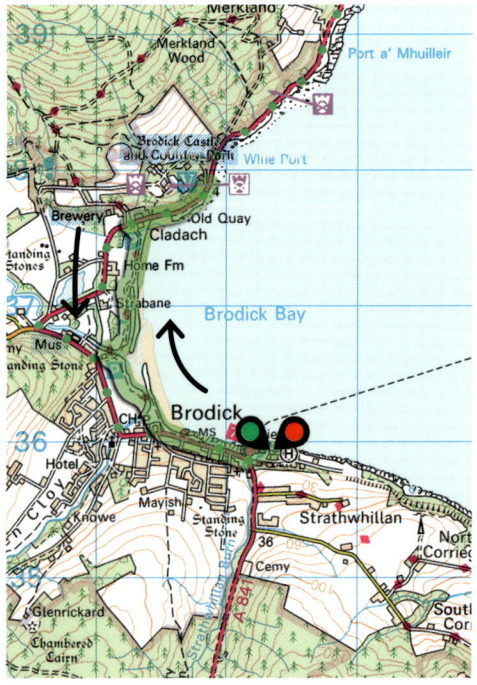

1

SCOTLAND

77 Loch Tanna

CATEGORY **Medium**   DISTANCE **14km**
ASCENT **340m**   START/FINISH **Catacol**   PUBLIC TRANSPORT **Both ways: bus to/from Catacol**

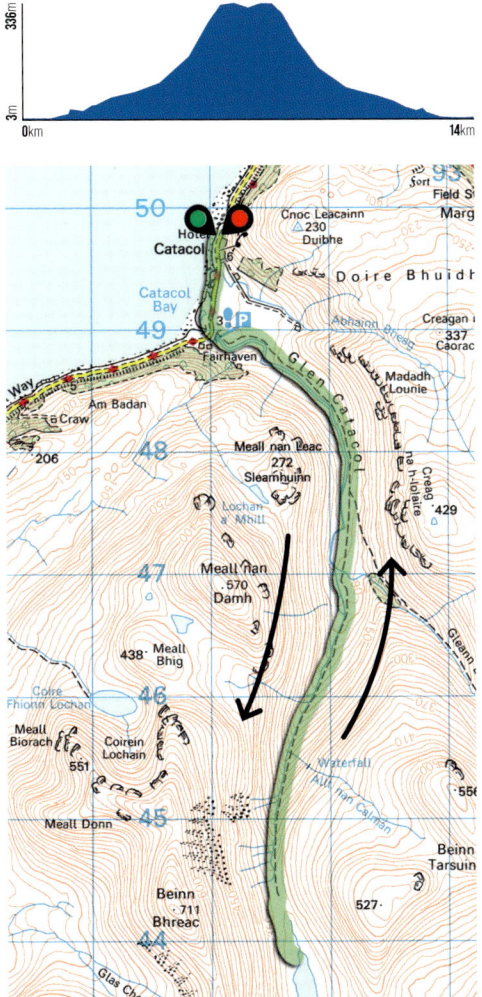

This out-and-back route takes you from the village of Catacol on Arran's north-west coast to Loch Tanna which is the island's most remote loch, as well as its biggest. Out-and-back routes can sometimes feel a little repetitive, but you don't have to worry about that here. On the way out you'll enjoy views into the depths of Glen Catacol, dotted with purple heather during the summer months, before ascending past the waterfall of Allt nan Calman, which has a plunge pool to dip in if you're feeling brave. Loch Tanna offers another dipping opportunity, or just a spot to eat your lunch, before turning around and beginning your return journey, the coast growing closer with every step.

An advance warning: you're highly likely to get wet feet on this one. But if you don't mind that, you could extend the route by diverting off to take in Loch na Davie (reputedly Scotland's purest water source) on the way back, before dropping down to Lochranza through Gleann Easan Biorach. This section does get extremely boggy though.

1 Laggan © Katie Perry   2 Lochranza Castle © Dave Parry   3 Laggan Cottage © Katie Perry

78 Sannox to Lochranza

CATEGORY **Medium**   DISTANCE **15km**
ASCENT **90m**   START **Sannox**   FINISH **Lochranza**
PUBLIC TRANSPORT **Outbound: bus to Sannox. Return: bus from Lochranza.**

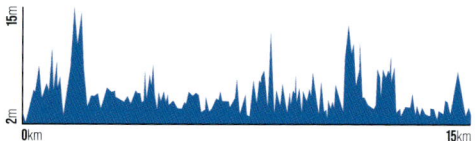

The stretch of coastline between Sannox and Lochranza is what made me fall in love with Arran on my first visit, when I followed its eastern edge while island hopping my way around the western coast of Scotland. It's often said to be the best part of the Arran Coastal Way (route 80), perhaps because while the rest of the route loosely tracks the road, this section veers away from it and hugs the north-eastern shoulder of the island. The lack of vehicular access gives you a real sense of remoteness. After all, nothing makes you feel quite as intrepid as going where four wheels can't.

From Sannox, you stick tightly to the coast almost the entire way except for a few short stretches of forestry track. There are several sights to cross off your Arran coastal bingo card along the way: the abandoned Laggan Cottage, which makes for a good spot to eat your lunch; the 18th-century ruins of Duchess Ann's salt pans, where sea water was heated to collect salt; and the Cock of Arran, a boulder which apparently looked remarkably like a crowing cockerel, until its head tragically eroded, which renders it a mere headless chicken these days.

I have two main memories from when I first did this section back in 2016. The first is getting cold feet about passing a particularly ferocious looking sheep (having mistaken it for a ram) and having to be escorted past it by some bemused walkers. The second is a very slow-going section through the An Scriodan boulder field. The good news is that the path through this bit has been recently improved, making it much easier, although there are still some slightly scrambly sections. Happily, once you're through the boulder field you're very close to Lochranza and you know what that means: the Sandwich Station.

79 Goatfell and Glen Rosa

CATEGORY **Long**   DISTANCE **21km**   ASCENT **910m**
START/FINISH **Brodick**   PUBLIC TRANSPORT
Both ways: bus to/from Brodick, if needed

Goatfell is the highest point on Arran, sitting at 874 metres above sea level. It's the tallest of the island's four Corbetts; unsurprisingly this accolade makes it probably the most popular hiking route on Arran, famed for its iconic summit views. The most straightforward route begins at Brodick Castle and involves an out-and-back up the main tourist track. Our route instead starts and finishes in Brodick itself, which avoids any extra bus faff and offers you the chance to incorporate both coast and mountain in the same loop (always a treat). You can easily get the bus around to the castle though, if you want to shave off a couple of kilometres.

The first kilometre or so follows the Fisherman's Walk, which you'll be familiar with if you've done route 76. Veering away from Brodick Bay, you'll head through the Cladach Visitor Centre, which is home to the Isle of Arran Brewery – worth a visit although perhaps not the most advisable place to start your hike! From Cladach the ascent begins, through forest then sparser birch woodland before the landscape opens up on to Goatfell itself. It's worth taking a few glances back as you climb, where you should be able to see Holy Island sitting in Lamlash Bay.

The path is quite straightforward to follow as it takes you up to the eastern shoulder of Goatfell and soon you'll swing left to begin the final part of the ascent, the trail growing increasingly rough underfoot. It's at this point that I found myself running straight into the low cloud that had been hovering just ahead the entire way and it'd be another hour or so before I could see anything more than a foot in front of me again.

Rumour has it that the views from the summit are pretty spectacular, with the neighbouring peaks jutting towards the sky and, supposedly, Ireland in the distance on a very clear day. Sadly, I can't confirm these views beyond the photos I've seen but I *can* tell you about the slightly sinister message etched into the trig point, promising 'I'll carry you in my soul for eternity'. Poetic as graffiti goes, I suppose.

From here, you have two options. Our loop takes you further north along the Goatfell ridge before dropping down into Glen Rosa. It's a fantastic route (which I can say with confidence as I finally got to see some of those famed landscapes when the cloud lifted a little) but does involve some scrambling and technical sections. It's worth doing if you're looking for a bigger challenge but only recommended for more experienced hillwalkers, comfortable with tricky terrain. Your other option is to retrace your steps back the way you came – hardly a consolation prize given that for the entire descent you get to enjoy the scenery you previously had your back to.

For those continuing on, you need to pick your lines carefully. I veered off route a few times and found myself unnecessarily scrambling over some more sketchy parts of the ridge, which I wouldn't recommend. The left-hand side of the rocky column leading to the summit of North Goatfell is less exposed, so try to stick to this side. It was here that the cloud lifted for me, and it was pretty incredible seeing the granite edges of the surrounding ridges become visible, with glimpses of the sea

to my left and right. That might be my favourite thing about exploring a smaller island – the perspective you gain when you're up high and can see the entire breadth of the island at once.

From North Goatfell your descent begins, first scrambling down to the saddle before eventually picking up a track on your left through Glen Rosa. That's the hard part done, and runners will happily be able to run again, the need for three points of contact over. Look out for the blue pools on your way down the valley. I'm gutted to have missed them as reputedly they're amongst the best wild swimming spots in the whole of the UK. Just another reason to go back?

1 The Sandwich Station, Lochranza **2** The pier at Corrie © Dave Parry
3 The Doon, north of Drumadoon Point © Katie Perry **4** Goatfell © Katie Perry

80 Arran Coastal Way

CATEGORY **Multi-day** DISTANCE **107km** ASCENT **1,050m** START/FINISH **Brodick, or anywhere on the coast**
MORE INFORMATION **www.coastalway.co.uk, www.scotlandsgreattrails.com**

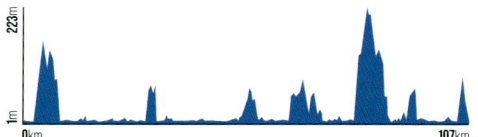

The Arran Coastal Way has been officially named as one of Scotland's Great Trails and for good reason. This 107-kilometre circular route allows you to do a lap of the entire island if you like. Alternatively, you can pick any number of sections to have a go at individually and use Arran's coastal bus service to travel between start and finish points. It's typically split into eight sections of between 8 and 16 kilometres apiece but, as with all these longer routes, you can divide it up however you like. There are also some alternative routes, including Goatfell summit. Runners looking for a challenge might even like to have a go at doing it in one – the current fastest known time stands at 14 hours and 34 minutes by Matt Stapley, if you're looking for something to beat.

The beauty of traversing the whole island in sequence is that it allows you to immerse yourself in the coastal variety that Arran offers in a way that you perhaps don't appreciate otherwise. Heading anti-clockwise from Brodick you'll first move in the shadows of the towering peaks that dominate the north of the island, before moving towards Lochranza's ruined castle and resident seals. Passing the Pirnmill hills as you make your way to the south of the island, you'll soon reach Blackwaterfoot with its sandy beach and, I have it on good authority, excellent bakery ('Best bakery ever!', I quote from a stranger on Instagram). This area is steeped in history too; look out for Auchagallon Stone Circle Cairn and King's Cave. Looping back around the southern end of Arran you'll find a more lowland landscape, rich with coastal wildlife and views of neighbouring islands.

There's something satisfying about completing a lap of an island and the Arran Coastal Way gives you the ideal opportunity to do exactly that, no matter how long you decide to take over it.

If you liked this
One thing Scotland isn't short of is islands, many of which offer the same incredible mix of mountains and coast that Arran does. If you take the train to Oban from Glasgow, there are several islands you can take a ferry to from there, including the Isle of Mull. Mull has the highest peak of all the Scottish islands and their only Munro (excluding those on Skye), plus silver sand beaches and ample sea-life-spotting opportunities.

Western Highlands

> BASE LOCATION **Fort William**
>
> WHERE TO STAY **A range of self-catering accommodation and B&Bs in Fort William, including Fort William Backpackers hostel. For camping, either Ben Nevis Holiday Park or Glen Nevis Caravan and Camping Park are easily accessible by bus.**
>
> HOW TO GET THERE **Train to Fort William (including the Caledonian Sleeper from London)**

It feels impossible to write an adventure book without overusing the word 'rugged', but the Western Highlands truly do deserve it. I don't think it's an exaggeration to say that you could fill a whole lifetime with adventures in this area, losing yourself (hopefully not literally) in the thousands of kilometres of trails taking you up, down and around the towering peaks that this part of Scotland is famed for.

Our base location is Fort William. Home to the British Isles' tallest mountain and sitting beside Loch Linnhe, it's no surprise that the town has become one of Scotland's key adventure hubs, making it the perfect place from which to explore the Western Highlands. It's the final stop on the Caledonian Sleeper train, meaning you can fall asleep in London and wake up in the mountains, and once there you've got a good mix of adventures on your doorstep and local public transport connections to take you further afield. You're spoilt for choice when it comes to accommodation, supermarkets and places to eat. My top recommendation is The Ben Nevis Inn. It's a 40-minute walk out of town (right by the start of the main tourist track up to the pub's namesake peak) but with regular live music and a traditional menu of haggis, rumbledethumps and Highland venison, it offers a quintessential Scottish experience.

The biggest challenge for this chapter was narrowing it down to just five routes, but I've tried to balance bucket-list summits with pockets of peace and quiet and high mountain adventures with loch-side loops. If you're staying longer or looking to make a return visit, I recommend checking out *www.walkhighlands.co.uk* for more adventure inspiration, especially as they handily detail public transport options where they exist.

1 Corrour station **2** Fort William rainbow **3** Càrn Mòr Dearg Arête on Ben Nevis
4 Running on the West Highland Way **5** Devil's Ridge © Jon Barton **6** On the West Highland Way

1–2 Views of Loch Linnhe from Cow Hill

81 Cow Hill

CATEGORY **Short**   DISTANCE **7km**   ASCENT **300m**   START/FINISH **Fort William**

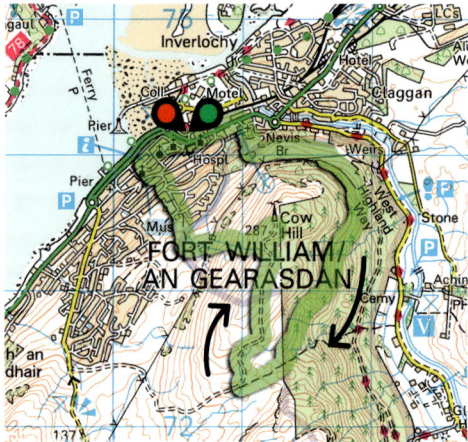

Cow Hill sits between Fort William and Ben Nevis. The downside of this is that it blocks the view of the latter from the former. The upside is that you're afforded some fantastic views in both directions when you climb it. This circular walk is a good one to get your legs moving after a long train journey and, if you're planning to do some of the longer routes in the book, being able to see in all directions gives you a good glimpse of what's to come. I climbed Cow Hill on the first day of a month-long trip around Scotland and it just made me super excited to get exploring.

At only 287 metres, Cow Hill is barely a bump compared to its neighbouring peaks but it does still have steep sections to be aware of. In particular, the descent is quite rough via this shorter route so you might prefer the longer but gentler version, which involves retracing your steps from the summit to pick up the main Cow Hill circular path (10 kilometres in total).

82 Loch Ossian

| CATEGORY **Medium** | DISTANCE **15km** | ASCENT **90m** | START/FINISH **Corrour station** | PUBLIC TRANSPORT Both ways: trains between Fort William and Corrour (50 minutes) |

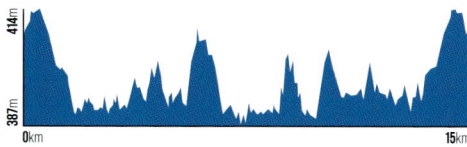

I could hardly write a book about public-transport-friendly adventures in the UK and not include one which uses what has been voted the most scenic rail journey *in the world*. Boarding the West Highland Line in Glasgow, you can leave the bustle of the sprawling city behind as you travel through some of Scotland's wildest terrain (and over the Glenfinnan Viaduct, made famous by the Harry Potter films) before terminating at the coast in Mallaig, where you can catch a ferry over to the Isle of Skye if you like. For a car-free deep dive into this corner of Scotland you could happily spend a week or two exploring along this line, hopping on and off wherever takes your fancy.

To reach the start of this route you'll only need to travel a few stops from Fort William to Corrour, but it's enough to see why this line was awarded such an accolade. The slow and steady climb through the Great Glen and up into the mountains gives you some incredible views, making it a journey you'll definitely want to bagsy the window seat for. Sitting at the edge of Rannoch Moor, Corrour is the UK's highest and, reputedly, most remote train station, with the only public access being via train, bike or foot (with a 30-kilometre walk in).

There are a number of isolated Corbetts and Munros in this area which you can tackle, but I love this low-level loop around Loch Ossian. To reach the water you'll need to follow a track for a kilometre or so from the station before picking up the trail which winds itself around the 5-kilometre-long loch. There's a decent footpath the whole way around, giving you the chance to experience the sort of isolation typically associated with more challenging routes while remaining on steadier terrain. As expected, the landscape of peaks layered behind the glimmering water is spectacular on a clear day but even in low cloud (as I experienced), there's a certain sort of atmospheric charm to Loch Ossian. As well as lots of wildlife to look out for, this is also a fantastic spot for star gazing with almost no light pollution.

You can do this route as a day trip but for a special overnight experience think about spending a night at Loch Ossian Youth Hostel. This eco-hostel is perched right on the water's edge and really tries to leave a positive impact on the environment it calls home, even down to bat-friendly paint. If you're brave, take a dip in the loch for your post-walk wash, as would have been guests' only option prior to hot showers being installed. These are now available thanks to solar and hydro power though.

I'd say that it's also practically mandatory to stop at Corrour Station House at some point which, despite the completely captive audience and zero competition, offers genuinely good, almost entirely locally sourced food. Meat eaters could easily exist on a diet of Corrour venison for three meals a day here, but the veggie options, cakes and breakfasts are great too. I had a particularly fantastic slice of banana bread, which was much needed after a very rainy loch-side walk.

1 Scramble in the Mamores range   2 Sunshine on the Ring of Steall   3 The Devil's Ridge

83 Devil's Ridge and the Mamores

CATEGORY **Long**   DISTANCE **21km**   ASCENT **1,200m**   START **Fort William**   FINISH **Kinlochleven**
PUBLIC TRANSPORT **Return: bus from Kinlochleven (50 minutes)**

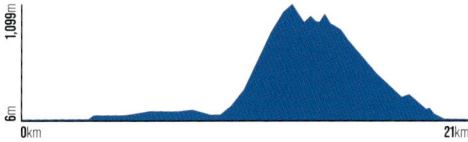

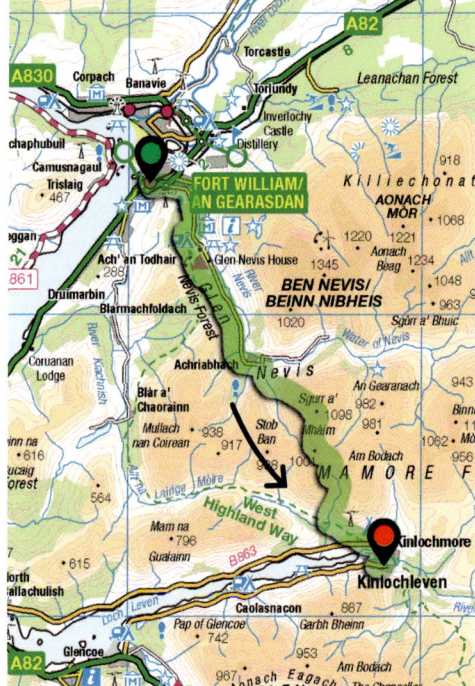

The Ring of Steall is a classic mountain route. Over the course of its 16 kilometres, you climb four Munros via scrambles across a number of narrow arêtes. The downside is that it's not the easiest one to do car-free, with the seasonal bus not giving you a huge window to complete the route in, and a long walk in or out otherwise. This alternative point-to-point option starts in Fort William and follows the West Highland Way for a few kilometres before diverting off to a high-level path. You'll then head up and over the Devil's Ridge, the most impressive part of the Ring of Steall route in my opinion, before dropping down to Kinlocheven, which has good bus links back to Fort William all year round.

The Devil's Ridge is home to Sgùrr a' Mhàim, which I once saw described as 'A massive lump of a mountain', a description I wouldn't argue with. I first climbed it during a longer day out attempting to do all of the Munros in the Mamores range ('attempt' being the operative word – I ran out of daylight and ended up cutting it short), and it goes down as one of my all-time best mountain moments. It had been a misty start to the day, and it was just as I tapped the summit of Sgùrr a' Mhàim that the last of the clouds blew over and the sunshine broke through. The picture I took looking back over the ridge after completing it is still my phone background. Just one of those moments where it all seems to happen at the right time – I'll keep my fingers crossed you have a similarly life-affirming experience!

84 Ben Nevis via the Càrn Mòr Dearg Arête

CATEGORY **Long**   DISTANCE **24km**   ASCENT **1,470m**   START/FINISH **Fort William**

Standing at 1,345 metres tall, Ben Nevis is the UK's highest mountain and, unsurprisingly, a bucket-list summit for many. The most popular route takes you up the so-called Tourist Path, beginning at Ben Nevis Visitor Centre. At nearly 17 kilometres long and with over 1,300 metres of climbing, this is a challenging day out and it's one you can do car-free by taking the seasonal N42 bus from Fort William to Glen Nevis (or with an additional 3-kilometre road walk at either end).

More experienced hillwalkers and fell runners might want to try this ascent via the Càrn Mòr Dearg Arête instead. It's a genuinely spectacular option with several advantages: you tick off another Munro (Càrn Mòr Dearg) and a Munro top (Càrn Dearg Meadhonach), you avoid many of the crowds and, as it begins in Fort William, you don't have to wait for any buses. The Càrn Mòr Dearg Arête is an exposed ridge though and traversing it requires some scrambling, so I'd recommend only tackling it if you feel confident in that environment.

But if you're prepared and have a good day for it, I think that this route is worth the extra effort a hundred times over. The approach to the summit of Càrn Mòr Dearg offers arguably some of the best views of Ben Nevis, with its huge bulk dominating the landscape and the dramatic cliffs of the North Face visible. You'll then move on from the ridgeline to the summit plateau and can enjoy a few moments as the highest person in the UK (whose feet are on solid ground, anyway), before descending via the Tourist Path. You then pick up the end of the West Highland Way, which follows the road at this point, back into Fort William where you'll find plenty of options for refuelling.

WALK BRITAIN

85 West Highland Way

| CATEGORY **Multi-day** DISTANCE **154km** ASCENT **2,810m** START **Milngavie** FINISH **Fort William** PUBLIC TRANSPORT **Outbound: train to Milngavie. Return: train from Fort William.** MORE INFORMATION www.westhighlandway.org, www.scotlandsgreattrails.com |

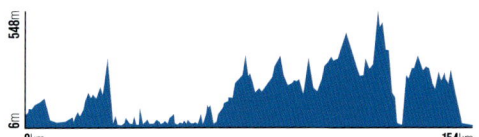

When the West Highland Way officially opened in 1980 it became Scotland's first designated long-distance route and today it's one of the most popular trails in Europe, and for good reason. Most commonly travelled south-to-north, the West Highland Way takes you on a 154-kilometre journey and offers a fantastic effort-to-reward balance. Mostly made up of good underfoot tracks and with a relatively small amount of climbing for a mountain route (less than 3,000 metres of elevation in total and a high point of 548 metres), you're afforded incredible views from start to finish as you wind your way through glens and between peaks.

Some of my best memories come from doing the West Highland Way with three friends. We crammed it into a three-day running mission which was heavy on the rain, the midges and the backpack chafing, yet more than five years on it's still the trip we laugh about the most.

If that's not the definition of some good type-2 fun then I'm not sure what is? And despite the rain we still got some solid glimpses of what lay beyond the clouds. Highlights included Loch Lomond opening out in front of us as we ran down to the water from Balmaha, singing Peter Andre's *Mysterious Girl* to get through a particularly rough patch just before the Glencoe Mountain Resort and flying down the descent from the Devil's Staircase to Kinlochleven. Lowlights included the slow, boulder-strewn path along the eastern shore of Loch Lomond, which was a bit of a soul destroyer at the end of a very long first day.

On the West Highland Way website you'll find sample itineraries splitting the route into five, six or seven days, but of course you can take as long as you like over it. Its popularity means this might not be the trail for you if you're looking for solitude, but it's ideal if you like a more social hiking experience or if you're looking for some safety in numbers on a solo trip. And with that popularity comes fantastic surrounding infrastructure. Make sure you carry some change and enjoy the contents of the many honesty boxes you'll find along the way.

If you liked this
Loch Lomond and the Trossachs National Park sits south of Fort William but offers a similar combination of big-loch-and-mountains (albeit the hills are slightly smaller than those around Fort William). Ben Lomond is the most southerly Munro and a popular one to tick off – in terms of transport, your best bet is to take the train from Glasgow to Tarbet then use the water taxi to cross to Rowardennan.

Cairngorms

> BASE LOCATION **Aviemore**
>
> WHERE TO STAY **A range of self-catering accommodation and B&Bs in Aviemore, including Aviemore Bunkhouse. Closest campsite is Oakwood Caravan and Camping Park (2km from Aviemore station; get the bus as far as Lochan Mor Lodge).**
>
> HOW TO GET THERE **Train to Aviemore (including the Caledonian Sleeper from London)**

The Cairngorms have plenty to brag about, as the UK's largest national park and home to five of Scotland's six tallest mountains. The area they cover is larger than the entire country of Luxembourg and contains more than one third of the UK's land above 600 metres. It's not all about the high ground though; within the Cairngorms you'll also find a quarter of Scotland's native forest, including the largest remnants of Scots pine, some of the country's longest and most impressive rivers, and wetlands providing a haven for many rare species. In fact – just to throw *another* stat at you – at least a quarter of all the rare and endangered species in the UK call the Cairngorms home.

But we all know that facts and figures alone don't make a good adventure. Perhaps the highest endorsement I can give the Cairngorms on that front is that I found it almost impossible to leave. Last September I headed to Scotland with basically no plan and wandered into a cafe in Aviemore to find a friend from university who I'd not seen for nearly ten years plastered in various purées as he attempted to feed Lola, his 9-month-old daughter. Ben immediately offered up his spare room and invited me to have dinner with him and his partner Katy – and a week later I was still there. From mountain days and bothy nights to river runs and loch swims, there was something about the Cairngorms that had me hooked. I even got to experience my very first cloud inversion here, a moment that I'll never forget.

Sitting on the eastern branch of the Caledonian Sleeper train with direct connections to Glasgow and Inverness, Aviemore makes a great base for a Cairngorms adventure. Stepping off the train you immediately have that feel of being in a mountain town – only enhanced by the mandatory uniform of trail shoes and a rainbow of down jackets. From here you can use local trains and buses to explore more. The number 30 bus will be your new best friend, running seven days a week between Aviemore and Cairngorm Mountain Resort.

1 Cairngorm plateau **2** Caledonian Pinewoods **3** Creag Bheag summit
4 Corrour bothy **5** Creag Bheag summit **6** Loch Gynack path

WALK BRITAIN

1 The River Spey near Aviemore © Kauai Colors/Shutterstock.com

86 Aviemore and the River Spey

CATEGORY **Short**   DISTANCE **7km**
ASCENT **40m**   START/FINISH **Aviemore**

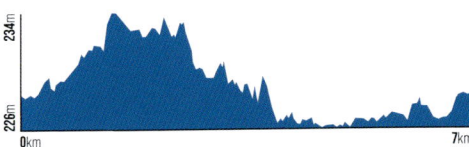

This route begins by following the Aviemore Orbital walk – this (mostly) waymarked path encircles the town and starts by taking you through Milton Wood. This provides some lovely woodland walking (or running) on forest tracks, with Scots pine and various other flora and fauna visible depending on when you visit. Aviemore has grown around the Orbital since it was first developed, meaning some parts of the walk are now more built-up, but our route adds in a section by the River Spey, arguably the highlight, and avoids the worst of that.

The Spey is Scotland's fastest flowing river; this section offers some fantastic viewpoints, both of the river itself and the mountains in the distance (snow-capped if you're lucky), before taking you back to the railway station. If you want to explore more of the Spey, check out the Speyside Way, one of Scotland's Great Trails, which loosely follows the Spey for 137 kilometres between Buckie and Newtonmore.

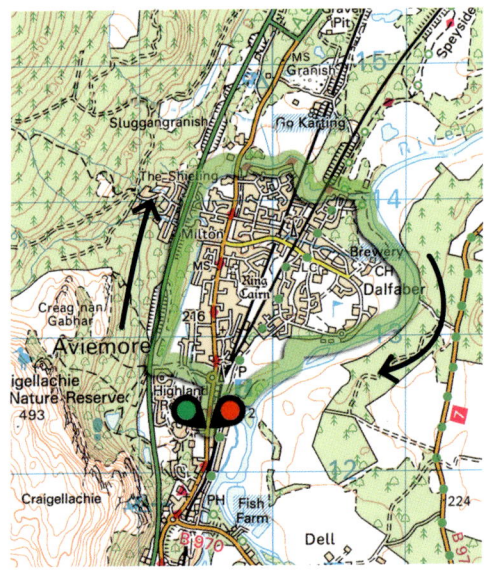

87 Creag Bheag and the Caledonian Pinewoods

CATEGORY **Medium**   DISTANCE **12km**   ASCENT **280m**   START/FINISH **Kingussie**   PUBLIC TRANSPORT **Both ways: trains or buses between Aviemore and Kingussie (15–25 minutes)**

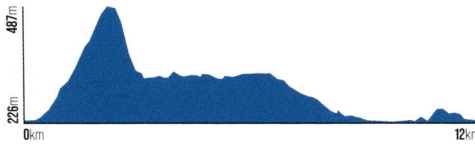

Even if you're not a tree enthusiast (my hand is up), you might have heard of the Caledonian Pinewoods. This ancient forest covered large parts of Scotland before human settlement and was the birthplace of the famous Scots pine, Scotland's only native timber-producing conifer tree. The Caledonian Pinewoods are much smaller today but still incredibly important as some of the UK's only true 'wild' forests and home to some of the UK's rarest wildlife.

Setting off from Kingussie, the first part of this circular route gives you a chance to roam through remnants of these ancient woodlands. The main way you can tell them apart from pine plantation is by the lack of uniformity in the spacing between the trees and you can identify Scots pine by its distinctive orange-brown, scaly bark. Make sure you look up and appreciate them towering above you.

Climbing up, you'll soon emerge from the woods and on to open moorland and up to the highest point of the route, Creag Bheag. At 487 metres, Creag Bheag only qualifies as a Marilyn but despite its low stature (compared to its Munro neighbours, at least), it gives some great views of the surrounding hills. Descending to Loch Gynack you'll pass a bench – make sure you bring a flask of something nice and linger here for a while. The trail hugs the loch for a time then becomes an absolute delight as it veers away from the water – a narrow path slicing between purple heather and green ferns.

Soon you'll veer left and head back towards Kingussie but if you want to go a little further, you can carry on heading west and loop around Newtonmore before returning. This extension gives you a chance to sample some of the Wildcat Trail.

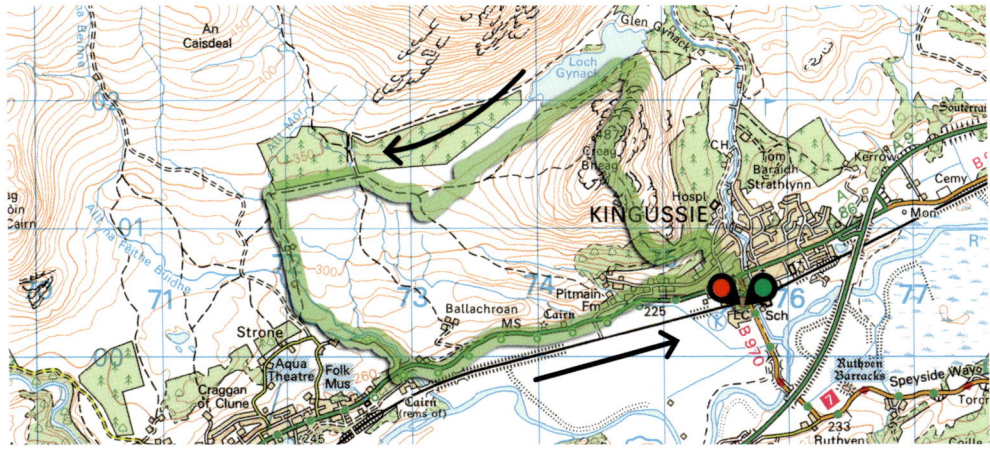

1 Cairngorm plateau 2 Macaroni cheese pie at the Cairngorm Mountain Resort 3 Well-kept trail in the Cairngorms

88 Cairn Gorm and Ben Macdui

CATEGORY **Long**   DISTANCE **18km**   ASCENT **870m**
START/FINISH **Cairngorm Mountain Resort**   PUBLIC TRANSPORT **Both ways: buses between Aviemore and Cairngorm Mountain Resort (25 minutes)**

As noted at the start of this section, if you're looking to explore the high mountains of the Cairngorms National Park then you'll want to get yourself well acquainted with the number 30 bus. It provides a link between Aviemore and the Cairngorm Mountain Resort, the starting point for probably some of the best hillwalking routes in the UK, that is, if this route around Cairn Gorm and Ben Macdui is anything to go by. It was my final route of the trip when I was seemingly incapable of prizing myself away from the Cairngorms and, as I wrote afterwards, comes highly recommended to anybody else who's lost their outdoors mojo, as I had prior to this day out. I seemingly remember listening to a lot of Natalie Imbruglia and eating vast amounts of Fruit Pastilles too which no doubt helped, and come as a strongly suggested accompaniment.

Anyway, the route. It feels notable as it takes in Ben Macdui, Britain's second tallest mountain, and Cairn Gorm, which is of course the national park's namesake. Despite standing at 1,309 and 1,245 metres respectively, this loop allows you to tick off both Munros while climbing less than 1,000 metres yourself, due to starting a significant way above sea level.

The Cairngorm plateau is a rolling arctic wilderness which, in winter, is typically the coldest place in Britain. This area is known for its rounded summits, the stumps of once much larger peaks, and these relatively gradual slopes are somewhat unusual in offering largely good underfoot conditions compared to many other hills of a comparative height. From memory, I was actually able to run fairly large parts of this route which, from somebody typically not great at very technical terrain, is high praise indeed.

The first peak of the day is Cairn Gorm which actually offers much more dramatic views than Ben Macdui, as you look over to the Northern Corries. Or perhaps I'm just saying that because by the time I reached the latter, visibility had worsened so that I couldn't really see anything. Hard to say, but the internet does seem to agree with that assessment. Enjoy the descent of the broad slopes of Cairn Gorm then follow the trails across the plateau before you begin what will become an out-and-back ascent of Ben Macdui, which is slow-going and rocky underfoot. There's not much of a visible path here and it's tricky to navigate, so be careful in poor conditions (and especially in winter).

Uphill done, it's time to enjoy your descent back to the mountain resort and what I would argue is the highlight of the day. You see, if Scotland was just a little bit further south (or my family were a bit further north) then I'd live here in a heartbeat and the national delicacy of macaroni cheese pies plays no small part in this. And easily the best one I've ever had was in the cafe at the Cairngorm Mountain Resort. Was it the pie, or was it the conditions? The jury remains out but all I know is that you truly can't beat a hot, cheesy pie in front of an open fire after several hours of being battered around in the wind and rain. Especially when, accompanying it, you have a hot chocolate with a mountain of whipped cream taller than the ones you've just climbed.

1 Chalamain Gap boulder field   **2** Purple heather in the Cairngorms   **3** Cairn Toul summit

89 Cairn Toul and Braeriach Traverse

CATEGORY **Challenge**   DISTANCE **36km**   ASCENT **1,570m**   START/FINISH **Sugar Bowl car park**
PUBLIC TRANSPORT **Both ways: buses between Aviemore and Cairngorm Mountain Resort (25 minutes)** – ask to stop at Sugar Bowl car park

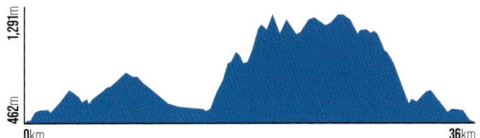

If you've done route 88 – Cairn Gorm and Ben Macdui – and you were blessed with a clear day, then you'll have seen the dramatic outline of Cairn Toul and Braeriach towering just across the Lairig Ghru (the hill pass which divides the national park). Now it's time to get a little closer to these peaks, which take the third and fourth spots on the list of the UK's tallest mountains (which is admittedly getting more airtime than I intended in this chapter, but who doesn't love a top five?). This is probably my favourite Scottish route, in no small part because it feels like a true epic. At 36 kilometres long and with over 1,500 metres of elevation this one isn't to be underestimated, but you do have the option of splitting it into two with a night at Corrour bothy, or a wild camp.

A word of warning: if you have a particular dislike of boulder fields, then this route probably isn't for you. Bookending your day is the Chalamain Gap, a narrow pass full of large boulders to be climbed up, down and around. Although it's a bit slow going navigating this section and you need to be careful, personally I'll take big boulders over small rocks and scree any day of the week. Gap crossed, you drop down into the Lairig Ghru and get to enjoy several kilometres sandwiched between the two imposing clusters of mountains on either side of you before reaching Corrour bothy and beginning the high mountain portion of the day.

The highlight of this day is, of course, the stretch between the two main peaks, as you follow the rim of these dramatic corries. This is a route that feels genuinely remote. Between the bothy and the second crossing of the Chalamain Gap – a stretch of around 15 kilometres, containing four Munros (The Devil's Point and Sgòr an Lochain Uaine, as well as Cairn Toul and Braeriach) – I only saw one other person, and this was a reasonably nice weekend day during the school holidays. It was hard not to feel vulnerable at times, but there's a sense of accomplishment in that too. As I walked back towards the Sugar Bowl, grateful to be on good trails again after the many, *many* boulders of the day, I thought about how a few years ago I'd have been neither fit enough nor competent enough to tackle a route like this, and there was something nice in recognising that. And something even nicer in celebrating with some chips back in Aviemore.

1 Dalnashallag Bothy **2** Castle ruin at Loch an Eilein
3 River Calder, Glen Banchor All photos © Katie Perry

90 East Highland Way

CATEGORY **Multi-day**   DISTANCE **132km**   ASCENT **1,570m**   START **Fort William**   FINISH **Aviemore**
PUBLIC TRANSPORT **Outbound: trains to Fort William. Return: trains from Aviemore.**

The East Highland Way is a 132-kilometre trail which was created with the aim of linking up the end of the West Highland Way in Fort William with the beginning of the Speyside Way in Aviemore. Travelling between the two towns, this unofficial long-distance route gives you the chance to experience the contrast between the Western Highlands and the Cairngorms, starting and finishing in the shadows of Scotland's two tallest mountains – Ben Nevis and Ben Macdui.

This is a largely low-level route, and you'll find yourself walking through forests, between mountains and past lochs. Both its beauty and its challenge lie in the remoteness of the trail. Unlike on the West Highland Way, you're unlikely to find yourself swept up with crowds – instead, you'll need to be happy getting your feet wet off trail and feel confident navigating pathless sections without waymarking. You'll never truly feel alone though as you happily spend the days looking for rare wildlife, from golden eagles and red squirrels to mountain hares and, if you're very lucky, a glimpse of the elusive Scottish wildcat.

If you liked this
One of the things that makes the Cairngorms so special, which hopefully you'll get a glimpse of through visiting, is that in places they offer a genuine feeling of wilderness which can be hard to come by in Britain. For more of this, have a look at the Kyle of Lochalsh train line which runs from Inverness. Alighting from any of the remote stops such as Achnasheen, Achnashellach and Strathcarron will all give you the chance to have a proper adventure, with towering Munros and deep lochs all around. Accommodation and amenities are limited in this area but don't forget that it's legal to wild camp in most parts of Scotland. So as long as you're stocked up on snacks, you're good to go.

More walking titles from Vertebrate Publishing

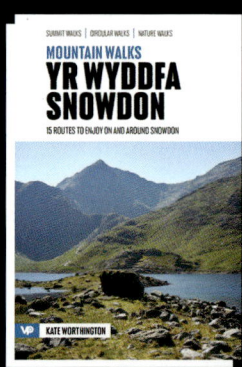 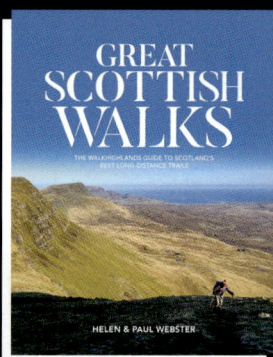 

  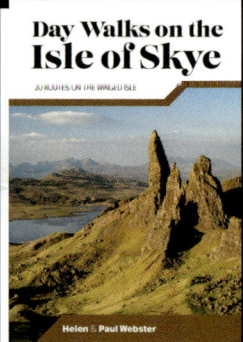

 inspiring adventure

Available from bookshops or direct
Sign up to our newsletter to save 25%
www.adventurebooks.com